INFOMANIA

⇒→ ═══► BY THE ◄═══ ←⇐

★ ★ Bathroom Readers' Institute ★ ★

Bathroom Readers' Press
Ashland, Oregon

Copyright © 2013 by the Bathroom Readers' Press
(a division of Portable Press). All rights reserved. No part of
this book may be used or reproduced in any manner whatsoever
without written permission, except in the case of brief
quotations embodied in critical articles or reviews.

"Bathroom Reader" and "Bathroom Readers' Institute" are
registered trademarks of Baker & Taylor. All rights reserved.

For information, write:
The Bathroom Readers' Institute
P.O. Box 1117
Ashland, OR 97520
www.bathroomreader.com

Cover and interior design by Andy Taray / Ohioboy.com

ISBN-10: 1-60710-561-6 / ISBN-13: 978-1-60710-561-9

Library of Congress Cataloging-in-Publication Data
Uncle John's infomania bathroom reader for kids only!
    p. cm.
ISBN 978-1-60710-561-9 (pbk.)
1. Wit and humor, juvenile. 2. Curiosities and wonders–Juvenile
literature. I. Bathroom Readers' Institute (Ashland, Or.) II. Title:
Infomania bathroom reader for kids only!
PN6166.U54 2013
081.02'07–dc23

                        2012043856

Printed in the United States of America
First Printing: February, 2013
        17 16 15 14 13   6 5 4 3 2 1

Our Readers Rave

*Some books print fancy reviews written by critics.
We'd rather share what our faithful fans have to say
about UNCLE JOHN'S BATHROOM READERS.
Thanks for reading!*

"I would like to thank *Uncle John's Bathroom Reader* and the Bathroom Reader's Institute. Recently, I qualified to attend the National History Bowl in Washington, D.C., and I couldn't have done it without your books. Thanks a lot, from one trivia geek to another."

—Brian C.

"Whenever I say something interesting, my mom will ask if I learned it from Uncle John (or *The Simpsons*)."

—Emily W.

"My friend in school was reading Bathroom Readers, so then I bought a couple. Now my mom says I'm threatening her with my intelligence."

—Chase O.

Thank You!

The Bathroom Readers' Institute sincerely thanks
the people whose advice and assistance
made this book possible.

GORDON JAVNA	ANNIE LAM
KIM T. GRISWELL	SYDNEY STANLEY
ANDY TARAY	LILIAN NORDLAND
JAY NEWMAN	GINGER WINTERS
BRIAN BOONE	JENNIFER FREDERICK
TRINA JANSSEN	ERIN CORBIN
MELINDA ALLMAN	R. R. DONNELLEY
JOANN PADGETT	PUBLISHERS GROUP WEST
AARON GUZMAN	THE EVO'S GANG
MONICA MAESTAS	FELIX THE DOG
MANA MANZAVI	THOMAS CRAPPER

Thanks to all the kids who have written to the BRI.
Without you, the FOR KIDS ONLY series would never
have happened. If you'd like to be part of shaping
future books, send us your ideas at:
BRI, P.O. Box 1117, Ashland, Oregon 97520.

Table of Contents

AN IMPORTANT MESSAGE FROM UNCLE JOHN...

Since you picked up this book, you could be one of a select group of kids with a condition known as *infomania*. Infomania makes you crave information. You want to know how **hippos brush their teeth**, which **ants explode on contact**, and who would **eat chocolate-covered garlic balls**?

To find out if you have infomania, answer these easy questions:

1. Are you, in fact, a kid?
(Good. This book is FOR KIDS ONLY!)

2. Do you want to amaze your friends, parents, and teachers with all the cool stuff stuffed in your brain?

3. Would you like to know if earthquakes are caused by catfish wiggling their tails?

If you answered "yes" to at least two of these questions, the info-nuts at the Bathroom Readers' Institute salute you! You are now an official Uncle John's Certified Infomaniac!

Go with the flow...
—Uncle John

CHAPTER 1

WORLDWIDE WEIRD

--- FUN FACT ---

THE LOCH NESS MONSTER IS A $50 MILLION-A-YEAR
BUSINESS IN SCOTLAND.

WEIRD MONGOLIA: With an average of only 4.7 people per square mile, Mongolia is the world's most sparsely populated country. It is also the only country in the world where horses outnumber people.

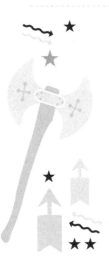

DYE, YOU SAXON PUNKS! When the Germanic Saxons invaded Britain 2,500 years ago, they sported colors meant to terrify. They went into battle with hair and beards dyed bright green, orange, red, and blue. They thought that made them look really scary and gave them an edge over their foes. Their scare tactics worked. (Of course, those two-handled battle-axes that could cleave a man in half probably helped.)

~ FUN FACT ~

IN SWITZERLAND, KIDS RECEIVE HOLIDAY EGGS FROM THE EASTER CUCKOO.

- The ancient Egyptians were the first people known to celebrate birthdays, starting around 3,000 B.C. But only the queen and male members of the royal family were honored.

- The ancient Greeks expanded the concept a little. They celebrated the birthdays of all adult males, and they kept on celebrating, even after a man had died. Women's and children's birthdays were considered too unimportant to observe.

- The Greeks got the idea of birthday cakes from the Persians. Then they added birthday candles to the party. (The candles symbolized moonlight and may have been used to honor Artemis, goddess of the moon.)

- In the Middle Ages, German peasants became the first to celebrate the birthdays of everyone in the family. *Kinderfestes*, children's birthday parties, were especially important. They were the forerunner to the kid's parties we have now.

EGOS ARE US

Dictators often give themselves long flowery titles that—they think—describe their amazing greatness. (*All hail Uncle John, Lord of the Porcelain Throne and Grand Master of Flushery!*)

- **Idi Amin, President of Uganda (1977–79)** had the official title, "His Excellency President for Life, Field Marshal Al Hadji Doctor Idi Amin Dada, VC, DSO, MC, Lord of the Beasts of the Earth and Fishes of the Sea and Conqueror of the British Empire in Africa in General and Uganda in Particular and the Most Ubiquitous of all King of Scotland dictators."

- **Muammar al-Gaddafi, President of Libya (1969–2011)** had the official title, "Brother

Leader, Guide of the First of September Great Revolution of the Socialist People's Libyan Arab Jamahiriya."

- **Joseph-Désiré Mobutu, President of Zaire (1965–97)** had the official title, "The all-powerful warrior who, because of his endurance and inflexible will to win, will go from conquest to conquest, leaving fire in his wake."

- **Kim Jong-Il, Supreme Leader of North Korea (1994–present)** is commonly called "Great Leader" but has many other grand titles:
—"Dear Leader, who is a perfect incarnation of the appearance that a leader should have;"
—"Guiding Star of the 21st Century;"
—"Sun of the Communist Future;"
—"Invincible and Iron-Willed Commander;"
—"Shining star of Paektu Mountain;" and
—"Glorious General, Who Descended from Heaven."

Welcome to Sealand

What if your family owned its own country?

CROWNED PRINCE

On September 2, 1967, a former British Army major named Paddy Roy Bates moved his family to an abandoned concrete and steel anti-aircraft platform six miles off the coast of England. The British government had built the platform (and several others) in the North Sea to defend its coasts from German invaders during World War II. They built them illegally...in international waters.

Bates declared his family's new home "the country of Sealand." He crowned himself H.R.H (His Royal Highness) Prince Roy of Sealand. His wife became Princess Joan and his son, Michael, became Prince Regent. The self-made ruler created postage stamps, passports, and even money—the Sealand dollar. And he gave the new country its own motto: "From the Sea, Freedom."

BOMBS AWAY

Prince Roy soon discovered that once you start your own country, you risk opposition from real-life governments. The British Royal Navy showed up. First, they dropped explosives on all of the other illegally built platforms. The massive structures blasted hundreds of feet into the air. Then the helicopters that had carried the explosives buzzed Sealand. The navy tug that had carried the demolition crew passed close to Sealand's platform and the men aboard shouted, "You're next!"

THE COURT RULES

H.R.H. Roy fired warning shots across the bow of the navy boat and it roared away. Instead of fighting it out with Bates, the British government looked to the courts to evict the family from the platform. A judge ruled that British authorities had no jurisdiction over Sealand because it was outside British territorial waters. Prince Roy ruled his strange little country for 30 years before turning it over to his son and heir.

VEGGIE BOMBS!

In 2003, an Italian woman was peeling an artichoke when it suddenly gave off a spark. Next, it spurted a little flame. And then...it exploded in a fiery cloud. Police rushed to the scene. They assumed the explodi-choke was the work of an Italian terrorist known to plant bombs in vegetables at Italian supermarkets. Not so. Testing showed no sign of explosives. Apparently it was a naturally-occuring exploding artichoke.

"Never be flippantly rude to elderly strangers in foreign hotels. They always turn out to be the King of Sweden."—Hector Hugh Munro

GOODBYE SMURFS: Belgium is the birthplace of those cute little blue guys known as Smurfs. In 2005, UNICEF, a children's rights group, aired an ad on Belgian TV. The ad showed the entire Smurf village being wiped out by warplanes. Only one Smurf survived: a crying baby. The final line read, "Don't let war affect the lives of children."

GETTING CLOSER TO JAPAN

On March 11, 2011, a magnitude-8.9 earthquake
rocked northern Japan. Two hundred and fifty
miles of coast dropped two feet, and a 500-mile-
per-hour tsunami (giant wave) rushed onshore.
The quake happened where the Pacific and North
American tectonic plates meet offshore. The
rupture was huge: 290 kilometers (180 miles) long
and 80 kilometers across (nearly 50 miles). The
result: parts of Japan are now 13 feet closer to the
U.S. than before the massive quake. The quake
also tilted the Earth's axis slightly and shortened
the day by 1.8 millionths of a second.

~~~→ FUN FACT ←~~~

IN 1994, THE JAPANESE METEOROLOGICAL AGENCY ENDED
A 7-YEAR STUDY INTO WHETHER OR NOT EARTHQUAKES ARE
CAUSED BY CATFISH WIGGLING THEIR TAILS. WHAT THEY
FOUND? NO...THEY'RE NOT.

- In 16th-century Europe, tooth dyeing was popular among upper-class women. In Italy, red and green were the most popular colors. Russian women favored black.

- Queen Elizabeth I (1533–1603) had red hair that started a hair-dyeing fad. Using a mixture of lead, quicklime, and sulfur, women dyed their hair to match the queen's. High-ranking men dyed theirs auburn, and some male courtiers dyed their beards as well. Loyalty, however, came with side effects: nausea, headaches, nosebleeds, and, thanks to the lead, kidney failure and death.

- Believe it or not, the fad of wearing oversized, low-riding pants started in U.S. prisons. In the late 1980s, many prisons banned the wearing of belts. Because standard-issue prison pants were often too big for inmates, they sagged. The style found its way into pop culture through rap music, caught on with teens, and became a multi-billion dollar industry.

UNITED STATES OF ODD

IT'S OFFICIAL: Every state has a motto, but some states have a few odder "official" items. Georgia has an official possum (Pogo, from the comic strip of that name); Maryland has an official exercise (walking); Texas has an official vehicle (the chuck wagon); and Washington has an official rock song ("Louie Louie").

THE WOLVERINE STATE: Pound for pound, the wolverine is one of the world's most powerful predators. A full-grown wolverine would only come up to a man's knees, but these vicious animals can bring down a caribou or drive away an entire wolf pack. Native Americans may have been the first to compare Michigan pioneers to wolverines. To the natives, the settlers' greed for land was like the wolverine's bloodthirsty hunt for food. Michigan is proud of the state's identity as the mighty "Wolverine State." (By the way, wolverines are weasels. Big weasels—in fact, the biggest— but weasels all the same.)

TRUTH-QUAKE: For a long time, people have worried that one day earthquake-prone California might fall into the ocean. True? No.

Most earthquakes happen along fault lines, breaks or fractures in the ground where Earth's tectonic plates move or shift. Geologists estimate as many as 15,000 faults in California. That's pretty shaky ground. But most of these faults are too small to cause much damage.

Many California quakes happen along the San Andreas Fault. It runs from the Mojave Desert to the San Francisco Peninsula, and the movement is horizontal. This means that Los Angeles and San Francisco are grinding toward each other at about 46 millimeters a year (about the size of two quarters laid side-by-side).

So, someday, your great-great-great-great-great-grandkids might be able to see the Golden Gate Bridge from the Hollywood Hills, but California will never fall into the ocean.

"California is a fine place to live. If you happen to be an orange."

—Fred Allen

- In **Arizona** it's illegal for a donkey to sleep in a bathtub.

- It's against the law to ride a merry-go-round on Sunday in **Idaho**.

- Cucumber littering is illegal in **New Jersey**.

- Drawing funny faces on window shades is against the law in **Montana**.

- In **Tennessee** it's illegal to drive a car while sleeping.

- A dead person cannot serve on a jury in **Oregon**.

- In **Alaska**, it's illegal to push a live moose out of a moving airplane.

PRESIDENTIAL CROOKS

Even U.S. presidents mess up sometimes. On a visit to France, Thomas Jefferson stuffed rice seeds into his pockets to take home to America. Smuggling was a capital offense in France. If caught, he could have been put to death.

On his way home from a friend's house, Franklin Pierce ran over an old woman with his carriage. He was arrested, but when the police realized the man in the cuffs was the President, they let him go.

Richard Nixon was arrested while in college because he sneaked into a movie theater without buying a ticket. He got away with it by calling up a judge who had gone to his college.

～ FUN FACT ～
IN THE UNITED STATES, DOGS
PRODUCE MORE THAN 5,000 TONS OF POO EVERY DAY.

THE BADLANDS: The Sioux thought the South Dakota territory was "bad" because of its rugged terrain and lack of water. They called it *Mako Sica*, or "land-bad."

"In the United States anyone can become President. That's the problem."—George Carlin

BALLOONS HO! The most common vehicle used on the Oregon Trail—the route many 19th-century pioneers took from the East to the West Coast—was the prairie schooner, a light, covered wagon. But they also used everything from wheelbarrows to handcarts to wind-powered wagons to make the trip. One inventor even tried to fly settlers to Oregon. In 1849, a man named Rufus Porter advertised that he could use balloons to carry people over the mountains. About 200 people signed up for the trip, but Porter ran out of money before he could make even one flight.

THE BEDBUG STATE: New York City has hundreds of thousands of apartments packed tightly together. Between 2009–2011 the city had a fullblown bedbug epidemic. One out of every five New Yorkers had bedbugs in their homes.

Bedbugs are tiny—only a few millimeters long—and they're thin as a business card. It's easy for them to slip through cracks from one building to another. They come out at night and they feed…on human blood.

New York City bedbugs are 250 times more resistant to standard pesticides than Florida bedbugs. They can live for weeks without water and months without food. And being rich or famous offers no protection. Former President Bill Clinton's Harlem office had them. So did the Empire State Building, the Waldorf-Astoria Hotel, and the Metropolitan Opera House.

~~~→ FUN FACT ←~~~

CENTERVILLE, OHIO, IS OFTEN CALLED "THE GEOGRAPHIC CENTER OF THE UNITED STATES." BUT IT'S NOT—THE REAL GEOGRAPHIC CENTER IS A HOG FARM NEAR LEBANON, KANSAS.

State capitals, birds, flowers...forget about 'em! This list offers one weird or embarrassing fact about every state in the U.S.

ALABAMA: Holds an annual casket race

ALASKA: Has the most heliports

ARIZONA: Famous for the London Bridge (shipped stone-by-stone from London and reconstructed in Lake Havasu City)

ARKANSAS: Holds the record for the most *E. coli* infections spread by petting zoos

CALIFORNIA: Most air pollution and roller coasters

COLORADO: Home of the Great Christmas Fruitcake Toss

CONNECTICUT: Most visits to the dentist

DELAWARE: Winnie-the-Pooh lived in the Thousand Acre Wood; this state has a Thousand Acre Marsh

FLORIDA: Installed the first bank ATM especially for roller bladers

GEORGIA: Known for having corrupt judges and politicians

HAWAII: World's wettest place (Mount Waialeale)

IDAHO: Has the words "Famous Potatoes" on car license plates

ILLINOIS: Popcorn is the "official state food"

INDIANA: Makes the most elevators

IOWA: Has more residents over age 85

KANSAS: Largest population of prairie chickens (wild grouse)

KENTUCKY: Has the only waterfall in the world with a regular "moonbow"

LOUISIANA: Tallest State Capitol (34 floors)

MAINE: Illegal to catch lobster with bare hands

MARYLAND: Most movie bootlegging

MASSACHUSETTS: Official state children's book, *Make Way for Ducklings*

MICHIGAN: Highest navy bean production

MINNESOTA: Most tornadoes

MISSISSIPPI: Most obesity

MISSOURI: Home of the most powerful earthquake in U.S. history

MONTANA: Elk, deer, and antelope outnumber humans

NEBRASKA: Birthplace of the Reuben sandwich

NEVADA: Gold mining

NEW HAMPSHIRE: Skin cancer for women

NEW JERSEY: Most millionaires

NEW MEXICO: Most children who drink alcohol

NEW YORK: Longest daily commutes

NORTH CAROLINA: Most kinds of salamanders

NORTH DAKOTA: Lowest rate of seat belt use

OHIO: Has more library visits than other states

OKLAHOMA: Because of the state's shape on a map, it has been called "the nation's meat cleaver"

OREGON: Largest homeless population

PENNSYLVANIA: Lots of UFO sightings

RHODE ISLAND: More drive-in movie theaters

SOUTH CAROLINA: Lowest gas prices

SOUTH DAKOTA: Highest rate of Facebook use

TENNESSEE: Turtle Capital of the World, with thousands of sliders, stinkpots, mud, and map turtles

TEXAS: Home of the world's largest rattlesnake roundup

UTAH: Birthplace of notorious western outlaw, Butch Cassidy

VERMONT: More children read to daily

VIRGINIA: Places on National Historic Register

WASHINGTON: Largest (nonmilitary) fleet of ferries

WEST VIRGINIA: Most heart attacks

WISCONSIN: The Troll Capital of the World

WYOMING: Most injuries from lightning strikes

Last Stand

The last battle of the Civil War happened in
Texas...a month *after* the war officially ended.

On April 9, 1865, Confederate general Robert E. Lee
surrendered to Union general Ulysses S. Grant at
Appomattox Courthouse in Virginia. That
officially ended the war between the states.
Unfortunately, Texas didn't get the memo.

At the southernmost tip of Texas another
battle took place. Union commander Colonel
Theodore Barrett ordered his men to attack an
encampment of Confederate troops at Palmito
Ranch near Brownsville. Historians are still
puzzled about why Barrett attacked. At the time,
forces on both sides in Texas had a "gentleman's
agreement" to keep out of each others' hair.

Whatever the reason, on May 11, 1865, Union
troops advanced on Rebel forces led by Colonel
"Rip" Ford. Ford and his men were in the dark
about the status of the war—they didn't know
they'd already been beaten. When Union troops
showed up at Palmito Ranch, these rebels weren't

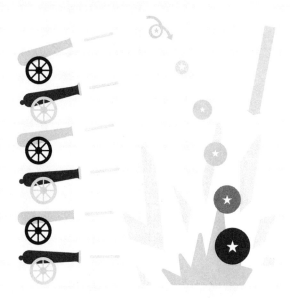

in a surrendering frame of mind. Ford blasted away with six cannons and led his men in a two-pronged attack on Union forces. They routed Barrett's troops and won the battle.

Union troops suffered 115 casualties, including at least 30 dead. Confederate forces also had dozens of injuries, but no deaths. Union prisoners captured during the battle spoiled the Rebels' win. How? They told the colonel and his men that the Civil War had ended before the battle began.

Myth-America

MYTH: Witches were burned at the stake during the Salem witch trials of 1692.

TRUTH: A hundred and fifty men and women were arrested under suspicion of witchcraft. In all, 19 people and two dogs were put to death as "witches and warlocks." But they weren't burned. Eighteen were hanged and one person was crushed to death by stones. Ten others were convicted, but not put to death, before the governor of Massachusetts dissolved the witch court. The judges didn't mind: They were running out of people to accuse.

MYTH: The westward expansion of the 1800s offered American pioneers millions of acres of fertile farmland.

TRUTH: The American frontier was not an organized democracy in which every "sodbuster" could own a piece of land. The money of big corporations dominated the West, even then. Although the federal government did permit pioneers to stake large claims in the Great Plains, the climate and soil were so dry it was almost impossible for settlers to raise crops or maintain livestock. To escape starvation, most pioneers had to sell their land to corporations. In return, the corporations gave them low-paying jobs as miners or farmhands. By the 1890s, almost 90% of the farmland west of the Mississippi River was owned by corporations.

MYTH: The American bald eagle, symbol of the United States, is a noble creature.

TRUTH: Benjamin Franklin called the American bald eagle "a bird of bad moral character." (He thought the turkey should be America's national symbol.) Franklin may have had a point. The American bald eagle is aggressive. Since the species was removed from the endangered species list in the late 1990s, the birds have been using their large talons and sharp beaks to attack fishermen and picnickers. Eagles have also been known to snatch puppies from suburban backyards, terrifying residents.

Milton Hershey got his first taste of candy making as a teen. At age 18 he became an apprentice to a candy maker in Lancaster, Pennsylvania. That was in 1875. By 1894 he had founded the Hershey Chocolate Company in his hometown of Derry, Pennsylvania.

The chocolate-making business made Hershey one of the richest men in the country. He decided to use some of that money to make sure the workers who had helped build his company enjoyed life. He created an entire community around his candy factory. First he built homes and a public transportation system. Then he added the fun: a park, a swimming pool, a bandstand, a bowling alley, and a carousel.

Over time, Hershey, Pennsylvania, became the unofficial "chocolate capital of the world" and "the sweetest place on Earth." It is now home to a 100-acre theme park, a zoo, and a chocolate spa where guests can take a whipped-cocoa bath.

CHAPTER 3

THE FIRST...

--- FUN FACT ---

IN 1927, BILLY POOGLE BECAME THE FIRST PERSON TO DIVE
FROM A 90-FOOT TOWER...INTO A PRUNE DANISH.

FIRST AGAINST SLAVERY: The first public protest against slavery took place in Germantown, Pennsylvania, in 1688. From the United State's earliest days, Philadelphia's abolitionists (anti-slavers) were a thorn in the side of slaveholders. One famous slave holder—none other than George Washington—complained that while he was on a trip to Philadelphia, a Quaker "stole" one of his slaves in order to free him.

UP, UP, AND... OOPS: E. R. Mumbord

designed the first helicopter that could lift a person off the ground. It had six propellers, each 25 feet in diameter. A 25-horsepower engine provided power. It worked fine, when the sun was shining. But if storm clouds rolled in, Mumbord's copter was in trouble. It was made of bamboo, not metal. Bamboo gets water-logged in the rain: not good if you're trying to stay above the ground, instead of crashing into it.

HEAR ABOUT THIS DIET? The first scientifically-planned slimming diet was created by an ear doctor in 1862. (You heard right...an ear doctor.) He developed the diet for an overweight undertaker named William Banting. Banting had to give up carbohydrates: potatoes, pies, sweets, and eat lean meat, fish, and fruit. He slimmed down from 203 lbs. to 153 lbs.

~~~→ FUN FACT ←~~~

IN 1995, FIRST LADY BARBARA BUSH, WIFE OF PRESIDENT GEORGE H. W. BUSH, WAS NAMED "FIRST LADY OF THE CENTURY" BY...*OUTLAW BIKER* MAGAZINE.

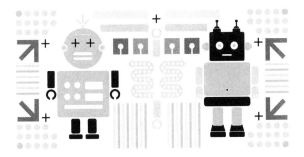

FORGOTTEN FIRSTS IN ROBOT HISTORY

• **1927:** "Maria," the first on-screen robot, appears in Fritz Lang's science-fiction movie *Metropolis*.

• **1940:** Isaac Asimov publishes "Robbie" (the first robot-themed fiction) in *Super Science Stories*.

• **1954:** George Devol receives the first patent for a robot. Five years later, his Unimate, a robotic arm, is installed at a General Motors plant in New Jersey.

• **1966:** A robot named Shakey, developed by the Stanford Research Institute, becomes the first robot that can actually react to its surroundings.

• **1983:** A robot called Ropet-HR lobbies Congress for increased spending in robot technology.

• **1984:** Rebecca the Robot runs for President of the United States as an independent candidate.

~~~> FIRST KISS

The first permanent U.S. movie theater opened in New Orleans in 1896. It had 400 seats and admission was just 10 cents. For an extra 10 cents, moviegoers could take a peek into the projection room and see the Edison Vitascope projector. A movie called *The Kiss* was a big attraction. Why? Because it featured the first onscreen kiss ever shown in America.

DON'T JUMP, MOM!

Fifteen-year-old Georgia Thompson of Henderson, North Carolina, joined a stunt parachute team in 1908. She made her first jump from a home-built biplane over Griffith Park, Los Angeles. That made Thompson the first woman to make a parachute jump from a plane. Women married young back then, and Thompson was already a mom when she made her historic leap.

"Some folks are wise, and some are otherwise."—Thomas Smollet

IN HOT PURSUIT: The first car involved in a police chase didn't even belong to a police department. It was borrowed. Sgt. McLeod of the Northamptonshire (England) County Police borrowed a Benz. Then he put the pedal to the metal and chased after a man selling forged tickets to see the Barnum and Bailey Circus. Sgt. McLeod's top speed in the Benz: 12 m.p.h.

The octothorp symbol (#) was first used in map-making to represent a village surrounded by 8 fields. (*Thorpe* meant village in Old Norse. And *octo* means eight.)

OOH...PRETTY: Before December 1882, strings of electric lights weren't used to make Christmas trees sparkle. Thomas Edison, the inventor of the first practical light bulb, made the first strand of electric lights. He strung them outside his Menlo Park Lab during the 1880

Christmas season. Two years later, Edison's business partner and friend, Edward H. Johnson, wired together 80 red, white, and blue light bulbs. He wound the strands around the Christmas tree in his New York City home.

LAWN MOWING: An English man named Edwin Budding invented the lawn mower in 1830. He got the idea from using a machine that sheared the nap off cloth. (Nap is the short fuzzy ends of fibers on the cloth's surface.) "Gentlemen," Budding said, "will find in my machine an amusing, useful, and healthful exercise." Just how "amusing" anyone found the contraption is questionable. It was heavy and the gears didn't work very well. But it was a lot better than mowing the lawn with a scythe. Imagine trying to get lawn mowing jobs while carrying a long stick with a sharp curved blade on one end. (You know...the kind the Grim Reaper carries around.)

~~~ FUN FACT ~~~

THE FIRST SIP OF KOOL-AID WAS TAKEN BY CHEMIST EDWIN PERKINS OF HASTINGS, NEBRASKA, IN 1927.

Batter Up!

Now that we have your attention, let's talk batting helmets. Believe it or not, before 1942 baseball players didn't wear batting helmets. In 1920, a player named Ray Chapman was hit in the head by a fastball. The ball split his skull and blood poured from his ears, nose, and mouth. Twelve hours later, Chapman was dead. There was still little interest in wearing helmets.

Then came Willie Wells, a hard-hitting shortstop from the Negro Leagues. Wells had a habit that made him especially vulnerable to being hit in the head. He hung his head over the plate when he batted. In 1942, Baltimore's Billy Byrd beaned Wells at Yankee Stadium and knocked him out. Two days later, Wells walked up to the plate wearing a miner's helmet.

Helmets made especially for the Major Leagues debuted in 1952. They became mandatory in 1971, with earflaps being required in 1983.

ONLY IN TEXAS: Idaho pilot Kenneth Arnold is often given credit for coining the term "flying saucer" in the late 1940s. But "flying saucer" actually dates back to a Texan named John Martin. On January 25, 1878, Martin was out hunting just south of the Red River. He was hoping to scare up a deer or some rabbits. Instead, he spotted "a dark object high in the northern sky." At first, the object seemed to be about the size of an orange. But it grew bigger...and bigger... and bigger...until it hovered right above Martin's head. Up close, it looked like a giant saucer flying high up in the sky.

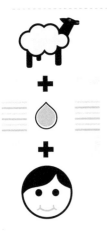

⤳ FIRST BLOOD

The first successful blood transfusion took place in 1667. A French doctor named Jean-Baptiste Denys injected blood into a 15-year-old boy. It wasn't human blood. It was sheep's blood. But the boy survived.

FIRST VIDEO GAME: In 1958, a physicist named William Higinbotham spent his work day coming up with "peaceful uses" for atomic energy. One day, he decided to create a game for people to play when they visited the lab. (He thought the exhibits the lab had for visitors were boring.)

He hooked up an old computer to a device called an *oscilloscope*, which had a screen. The game was simple: a ball of light bounced back and forth across a "net." (The net was just a short line made of light.) Players used control boxes to hit the ball back and forth over the net. Higinbotham called the game "Tennis for Two."

Visitors loved it and hundreds lined up to play. By 2001, Americans had spent $9.4 billion on video games and software. How much of that went to the inventor of the first video game? *Zilch. Zero. Nothing.* Higinbotham never made a penny from video games. He worked for a U.S. government lab. So even if he had patented his tennis game idea (he did not) the government would have owned the patent...and pocketed all the money.

First Million-Dollar Acting Contract (1921)
Paramount Studios paid comedian Roscoe "Fatty" Arbuckle $1 million a year for three years.

First 3D Movie (1953) *House of Wax* was the first 3D film from a major studio. The movie's director Andre De Toth had only one eye, so he couldn't see the 3D effects.

First computer-animated feature film (1995)
Pixar's *Toy Story* was the first cartoon movie to be drawn entirely by computer.

First All-Digital Movie (2002) *Star Wars Episode II: Attack of the Clones* directed by George Lucas.

CHAPTER 4

NATURE CALLS

AN ALLIGATOR'S BRAIN IS ABOUT THE SIZE
OF A POKER CHIP.

⟵ PULL UP THOSE PANTS! In the 1980s, a Russian biologist heard that people living on the Kamchatka Peninsula in northeast Russia had sighted a strange bear. They called it *irkuiem*, which means "trousers pulled down." They said the bear had bunches of fat that hung down between its rear legs and made it look like it was wearing falling-down trousers. The biologist suggested the animal might be a surviving strain of *Arctodus simus*, one of the largest bears that ever lived. Before it went extinct, the bear inhabited North America for millions of years, from Mississippi to Alaska—right across the land bridge from Russia, where the locals were telling their irkuiem stories.

~~ FUN FACT ~~

HIPPOS GET THEIR TEETH CLEANED BY CARP.
A FULL-GROWN HIPPO'S LIPS ARE ABOUT TWO-FEET WIDE,
AND ITS LOWER CANINES CAN BE THREE FEET LONG.

HAPPY SQUIRREL DAY! Christy Hargrove, a wildlife rehabilitator from Asheville, North Carolina, turned January 21 into a special day just for squirrels. The holiday started as a way to get local kids interested in the region's squirrel species, some of which are endangered. But Squirrel Appreciation Day has grown more and more popular at schools throughout the United States. Why is it in January? That's when food for squirrels is the most scarce, and kids are encouraged to put out seeds, nuts, or suet for them. The holiday is also a great way to share cool squirrel facts, like this one: The word "squirrel" goes back to the Greek *skiouros*, a combination of "shade" and "tail," which meant "creature who sits in the shadow of its tail."

POO FROGS: In Sri Lanka, an elephant researcher has found three types of frogs that live in elephant dung. Beetles, ants, spiders, and other insects live in the dung, too. So perhaps the frogs are just looking for a quick meal.

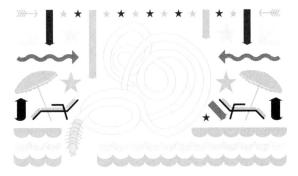

GIANT BEACH WORMS

If you're strolling down a beach in Australia, there might be huge carnivorous worms right under your feet. Giant beach worms spend their lives in the sand right at the shoreline, popping up when a wave recedes to search for whatever new organic matter the sea has brought in. If you watch closely, you can sometimes see their white, grublike heads—with little black legs attached to them—pop up out of the sand to grab something. How big is "giant"? They've been known to grow to more than six feet in length—and there can be tens of thousands of them under the sand on any given beach.

∼∼∼ WHAT A SHOCK!

In 2007, scientists in Thailand discovered a bright pink millipede, just over an inch long and covered in tiny spikes. The shocking pink dragon millipede spends most of its time foraging for decaying matter on top of leaf litter. That's odd behavior for a millipede—more so for a bright pink one! They usually hide under rocks, fallen logs, and leaves. Why? Because they're a common food for a wide variety of predators.

Turns out, the shocking pink dragon millipede doesn't have to worry. If something tries to eat it, it activates special glands in its body that produce cyanide gas. The millipede shoots the gas out of its mouth right at the predator and sends it quickly on its way.

Bonus Fact: Shocking pink dragon millipedes smell like almonds. That's because of the cyanide, which occurs naturally in almonds and gives them their distinctive odor.

THE HOAX IS ON YOU! In 1799, a sea captain sent George Shaw, curator of the Natural History Department of the British Museum, an animal carcass supposedly found in Australia. It looked like a mole with a bird's bill and beaver's tail attached. Shaw suspected a hoax. He thought swindlers had merged animals together and passed the whole off as a new species. His peers were equally skeptical. But as more specimens turned up, scientists were forced to believe in and categorize the new animal...and that's how the duck-billed platypus became legendary for being real.

SPONGIFORMA SQUAREPANTSII

San Francisco State University researcher Dennis Desjardin gave this mushroom species its name in 2011. Why? Because the mushroom not only looks like a sea sponge, when viewed under an electron microscope, it looks like the ocean floor where cartoon character SpongeBob SquarePants lives.

SPECTACLED BEARS: People climbing in the Andes of South America sometimes think they spot bears wearing glasses. Spectacled bears are black, with beige markings on their chests and faces. It's the marks on their faces that make them look as if they're wearing glasses. They weigh about 340 pounds on average and their diet includes fruit, nuts, honey, berries, corn. Cactus flowers are a favorite, but the bears have to climb cactuses to reach them. Spectacled bears eat some meat, most often in the form of rabbits, rodents, birds, and occasionally llamas. They build nestlike platforms in trees, using broken-off branches and leaves. And they spend a lot of time in those cozy tree houses.

~~~→ FUN FACT ←~~~

IN A TROPICAL RAINFOREST IT CAN TAKE A DROP OF RAIN MORE THAN 10 MINUTES TO REACH THE GROUND.

GREAT JUMPING ANTELOPES! The klipspringer, a small African antelope, can leap 30 feet straight up in the air. Africa's impala, a medium-size antelope, can leap 40 feet...sideways.

• The binturong, a small carnivore from tropical Southeast Asia, smells like buttered popcorn. The scent comes from a gland beneath the animal's tail.

• The eucalyptus leaves that koalas eat make them smell like cough drops or cold remedies.

• Swallowing a lot of skunk spray can cause temporary blindness, nausea, and even fainting. (A skunk's spray, by the way, is *phosphoric*, which means it glows in the dark.)

• When they sting, bees release pheromones that can smell like bananas.

• Africa's version of the skunk is the zorilla, or striped polecat. It protects itself like a skunk, by lifting its tail and spraying. The zorilla's spray is said to smell like vomit or really strong cat pee.

• When threatened, the tamandua, a type of anteater found in South America, releases a smelly spray to scare off predators. Locals call the female tamandua the "stinker of the forest."

• The male musk ox uses his urine to mark his trails and himself. He splashes his long, thick, woolly hair with it—especially in mating season.

• Bull elephants go through a periodic condition called *musth*, a surge in testosterone that lasts about a month. One of the signs of musth is a secretion that comes from a gland between the animal's eyes and ears. In young elephants, the musth smells like honey and will attract bees. But the older the elephant, the funkier and muskier the secretions become.

• The crested auklet, a seabird that lives mainly along the coast of Alaska, smells like tangerines. Researchers believe the scent is used for bonding, mating, and to repel parasites.

Talking Trees

These days, fantasy writers aren't the only ones who think trees can "talk" to each other. Here's what some scientists have to say.

Scientists from the National Center for Atmospheric Research studied trees in a California walnut grove. The area was in a drought, and the nights were very cold. The trees reacted by producing a chemical called *methyl salicylate*. It works on trees like aspirin does in humans: to relieve pain or discomfort. It also raises the trees' defenses against environmental dangers.

Not only did individual trees use the chemical to defend themselves, they released it into the air to warn nearby trees of the dangers. Those trees then began producing their own methyl salicylate. In other words, NCAR scientists believe that the trees "talked" to each other to warn about the environmental threats.

"We trees do what we can. We keep off strangers and the foolhardy; and we train and we teach, we walk and we weed."

—Treebeard the Ent, from J.R.R. Tolkien's *The Lord of the Rings*

Step 1: Make a fire ring.

Step 2: Gather what you need.

1

2

Pick a flat clear spot without overhanging tree branches. Clear all debris within a 10-foot diameter. Collect flat rocks—brick-sized or larger. Arrange them in a ring at the center of the clearing. The ring doesn't have to be big— just a few feet across is fine.

Place a bucket of water near your ring to douse flames when needed. Gather tinder (wood shavings or paper), kindling (fallen dry twigs or small branches), and fuelwood (dry wood about the thickness of your arm). Stack in separate piles, not too close to the ring.

Step 3: Make a lean-to.

Step 4: Add fuel and light it up!

3

4

Make a loose pile of tinder in the center of the ring. Stack pieces of kindling around the tinder, to form a tepee shape. Use thicker pieces of kindling as you add layers to the tepee. Finish with four or five pieces of fuelwood about as big around as your wrist.

Light the tinder beneath the teepee. Add larger pieces of wood as the fire gets going. When the tepee burns down to coals, add wood in crisscrossed layers, to allow air to feed the fire. And when you're ready to leave, douse the fire with the bucket of water. Make sure it's out!

The Vampire Finch

A small finch found on the Galápagos Islands has evolved some feeding habits that may send shivers down your spine.

GORY: The vampire finch usually eats seeds and insects. Sometimes it sucks the nectar from flowers. But every year, a long dry season makes these foods scarce. So the vampire finch must find other ways to feed its hunger. Most of the time, it heads straight for the nearest boobie. A boobie is a large seabird also found on the islands. Female boobies lay their eggs on the rocky ground. It's common for a vampire finch to sneak up behind a boobie as it lays an egg and drink the lubricating fluids that come out with the egg. That fluid is a good source of protein.

GORIER: Almost as soon as the vampire finch finishes eating the fluid, it steals the egg. The finches have learned to roll boobie eggs—which are nearly as large as they are—over little rocky drops to break them. Then they gobble up the nourishing insides.

GORIEST: Vampire finches also peck the wings and bodies of boobies and other seabirds until they bleed. And then...they drink their blood. Strangely, the seabirds let them do it. Biologists believe the reason for this bizarre behavior— the only example in all the bird world—is that it began with finches eating parasites off the bigger birds' skin. Over time, that evolved to pecking, then to bleeding—and then the vampire bird got its very deserved name.

"We hope that, when the insects take over the world, they will remember with gratitude how we took them on all our picnics."

—Bill Vaughan

THE TRUTH ABOUT QUICKSAND

You've probably seen old movies where an explorer gets lost in a jungle and steps in a patch of quicksand and then slowly sinks to his death. That's pure Hollywood myth. Quicksand is just sand mixed with groundwater. The sand might appear normal on the surface. If it has formed a crust, dried by air and sunlight, then the pool below will be hidden. But if you do get stuck in quicksand, it's not hard to escape. If you're not in up to your waist, just wade out. If it's deep, float. (Huh?) Your body is less dense than quicksand, so relax. Move slowly and work your way onto your back. Don't panic! If you flail your arms and legs you could work yourself in too deep. If that happens, you really could drown.

HOW MUCH GRASS DID DINOS EAT?

None. At least that's what paleontologists think. Dinosaurs lived until about 65 million years ago. There were cone-bearing trees and plenty of shrubs. But grass? According to fossil records, grasses didn't show up until after the dinosaurs were gone.

BLONDES HAVE MORE...BUG BITES!

Mosquitoes can sense the breath of animals from as far as 100 feet away. But once they get close, sight comes into play. The buzzy little blood-suckers notice contrast more than anything else. Since blonde hair stands out more than dark hair, blondes are more likely to get bitten.

> "The difference between genius and stupidity: Genius has limits."
> —Albert Einstein

CAN RATS VOMIT?

No, and they can't burp, either. Why not? Rats have a barrier between the stomach and esophagus. And they don't have muscles strong enough to open it. Since they can't barf up things that could kill them, rats have keen noses. Those noses can warn them if something is toxic. Rats are also very careful eaters. They take tiny bites and wait to see if anything bad happens. If so, they avoid that food in the future.

THE IMMORTAL SEA SQUIRT

Sea squirts may act more like potatoes than animals, but scientists have discovered an ability that makes them special. Older parts of a sea squirt get broken down and recycled to grow new and healthy parts. That means the sea squirt doesn't age the way other animals do. In theory, that means they could live forever.

SEA-ING THINGS: Dolphins sometimes play chase in long lines. (It looks like a snake dance or kids playing snap-the-whip.) Sailors who spot dolphin chases sometimes think they're seeing huge sea serpents.

CHAPTER 5

EATS &
TREATS

~~~ FUN FACT ~~~

THE AZTECS OFFERED THEIR GODS HUMAN SACRIFICES
AND...TAMALES.

FOAMING AT THE MOUTH: A chef in Spain found a way to make tastes stronger than ever. He condensed ingredients down and then put them into a special bottle charged with nitrous oxide cartridges (similar to a whipped cream container). So far, he has created three melt-in-your-mouth foams: espresso foam, mushroom foam, and beef foam.

~~~ GUMBUSTERS!
Love to chew gum but sick of finding it stuck to your shoe? Believe it or not there's someone geared up to keep that from happening. Gumbusters! They use a contraption similar to a rug cleaner to superheat the sticky goo so it can be easily washed or vacuumed off floors or sidewalks. Gumbusters are in great demand in most major cities (except in Singapore, where chewing gum is illegal).

BACON LOVERS: If you love bacon but want to avoid eating something nutritionists say isn't healthy, there's hope. Shake on bacon salt to make everything taste like bacon. Use bacon-flavored dental floss (because bacon tastes better than waxed string). And make friends with bacon action figures. They come in a set of two: the heroic, all-American, bacon strip-shaped "Mr. Bacon," and his nemesis, the evil, cube-shaped "Monsieur Tofu."

KENTUCKY FRIED CHINA

The first American fast-food restaurant opened in China in 1987. It was KFC (called Kentucky Fried Chicken at the time). Today, there are more than 1,000 KFC restaurants in China. The menu caters to local tastes, serving dishes such as rice, spinach, and tomato porridge.

10 THINGS ABOUT IRISH POTATOES

1. Before the 1600s, no one in Ireland had even heard of potatoes. They grew in South America and were brought to Ireland by explorers.

2. Enough potatoes can grow in a half-acre of boggy Irish soil to feed a family of six.

3. You can live on a diet of nothing but potatoes.

4. Irish workmen ate around 14 pounds of potatoes a day to stay healthy and active.

5. By the 1840s, about 3 million Irish were eating potatoes for breakfast, lunch, and dinner.

6. Potatoes kept people so healthy that the poor had more babies than ever before, doubling the country's population in only 50 years.

7. In 1845, potatoes made up 1/3 of Irish crops.

8. That same year, a fungus attacked the potato crop. The potatoes turned black, soft, and smelly and could not be eaten.

9. Between 500,000 and 1 million people starved to death. Another million left the country, many for the United States.

10. The Irish Potato Famine lasted until 1851.

THE SQUEAKY CHEESE MAN

According to legend, cheese was discovered thousands of years ago by a Middle Eastern nomad. He poured milk into his saddlebag, which was probably made from an animal's stomach and would have contained traces of the coagulating enzyme *rennin*. In the desert heat, the rennin would have curdled the milk into two parts: clotted solids and cloudy liquid.

The solids, when separated from the liquid *whey*, are the cheese curds. The curds can be formed into blocks or balls and aged to make cheese, or eaten as-is. If they're not pressed into blocks or balls, the air trapped inside the rubbery curds "squeak" when bitten. So sometimes they're sold as "squeaky cheese." In Wisconsin, the world's biggest cheese curd maker, squeaky cheese is often battered and deep-fried, and served as a snack or a side dish.

~~~ FUN FACT ~~~

THE PILGRIMS REFUSED TO EAT LOBSTERS BECAUSE THEY THOUGHT THEY WERE HUGE INSECTS.

FRANKENFOODS

Farmers have been creating new kinds of plants for hundreds of years. In the past, they used an old-fashioned method: cross-pollination. That means they mixed the pollen of similar plants to create a hybrid, a new kind of plant. Scientists now breed plants by manipulating their genes. And they don't just cross one plant with another: they mix plant genes with animals genes. So scientists creating "transgenic" plants may be more like Dr. Frankenstein than Old MacDonald. Here are a few examples of the "plants" they've already made, or are currently trying to create:

- tomatoes that have genes from an Arctic flounder to make them resistant to frost,

- corn crossed with genes from a bacterium to make it poisonous to insects,

- apples with a gene taken from a moth to make the apple tree resistent to fire blight (a disease that destroys millions of dollars worth of apples worldwide every year), and

- smart crops with a firefly gene that makes them glow when they need water.

In nature, transfer of genes happens only between closely-related species. The Sierra club, an organization that works to protect the environment, claims that "if we continue on our present path, we will eventually live in a genetically engineered world." Nature, as we know it, they claim, will cease to exist.

"A potato can cross with a different strain of potato but, in 10 million years of evolution, it has never crossed with a chicken. Genetic engineering shatters these natural species boundaries, with completely unpredictable results."—Michael Khoo (from a letter published in the *Toronto Globe and Mail*)

LUNCH IN SPACE: Despite the best efforts of NASA food scientists, what passed for food on early space flights...wasn't. Astronauts had to eat cubes textured like dog biscuits, freeze-dried powders as appetizing as desert dust, and tubes of gluey stuff that was like toothpaste, without that pleasant minty flavor. That may be why astronaut John Young smuggled a corned beef sandwich aboard a Gemini flight in 1965. Fellow astronaut Gus Grissom ate it, but Young was "officially reprimanded." NASA must have been pretty upset by the unauthorized sandwich—Young was the first astronaut to be reprimanded for anything.

~~~ FUN FACT ~~~

ANCIENT ROMAN BANQUET HALLS HAD "VOMITORIUMS" SO PEOPLE COULD KEEP EATING AFTER THEY WERE FULL.

SECRET INGREDIENTS: There are 38 ingredients in McDonald's Chicken McNuggets. Chicken is *not* at the top of the list. A McNugget is 56 percent corn products, and there's even a little TBHQ in them. What's that? Lighter fluid.

Mongolia. *Boodog*, the flesh of a goat broiled inside a bag made of the goat's dried skin. The goat is then barbecued or cooked with a blowtorch.

Belize. *Cena Molida*, a popular mixture that includes roasted, mashed cockroaches.

Ecuador. Fried guinea pig.

Portugal. *Tripe*, which is three of the four stomachs of a cow. It's really tough, so it has to be boiled until it's tender enough to chew.

The Netherlands. Salted horsemeat sandwiches.

The Philippines. Rat sausage.

Cambodia. Fried tarantulas seasoned with sugar, salt, and garlic.

Indonesia. Monkey toes.

Vietnam. Whole baby mice, each about an inch long, grilled, and served with a spicy dipping sauce.

U.S.A. *Burgoo*, mostly found in Kentucky, is a stew made with vegetables and squirrel brains.

HOW TO MAKE HAGGIS

The national dish of Scotland may be the world's most disgusting food. But if you happen to have a spare sheep's stomach, you might want to make it.

Step 1: Gather ingredients.   *Step 2: Boil and cook.*

You'll need a cleaned sheep's stomach, 1 lb. of sheep liver, 1 large chopped onion, 2 lbs. of dry oatmeal, 1 lb. of chopped suet (beef fat), 3 cups of beef stock, and 1/2 teaspoon of black pepper, cayenne, and salt.

Boil the liver and onion until the liver is cooked. Chop them up and mix them together. Lightly brown the oatmeal in a skillet, stirring constantly to prevent burning.

Step 3: Stuff the stomach.

Step 4: Poke it with a needle.

Mix all the ingredients together and stuff the sheep's stomach with it.

Sew the stomach up and prick it with the needle a few times so it won't burst while cooking. Slowly boil for four hours.

Battling Bakers

Most people think fortune cookies were invented in China, but they weren't. They were invented in California in the early 1900s. Two bakers—both of Asian descent—claim to have invented them.

A Japanese baker named Makoto Hagiwara said he sold the first fortune cookies at his tea shop in San Francisco sometime around 1915. (They had little thank you notes in them.)

A Chinese-American baker named George Jung said he made the first ones in 1918. He put verses in them and handed them out to jobless men near his bakery in Los Angeles.

In 1983, the two bakers took their argument to court. The judge ruled in favor of Hagiwara.

As for the first note-filled cakes, they were used in ancient Chinese parlor games. Players wrote wise and witty sayings on scraps of paper that were then inserted into twisted cakes. Later, Chinese monks rebelling against their Mongol rulers slipped messages into mooncakes, a sweet holiday dessert, and sold them to the people.

HOW FORTUNES GET INSIDE COOKIES

The cookie dough is flattened into circles and
then baked. While the baked cookie circles are
still warm, they're folded over with slips of paper
inside them. As the cookies cool, they harden into
their familiar shape.

BALLPARK BITES: It's not all hot dogs and sodas at major-league stadiums. Many stadiums offer local favorites like these:

- **Ichiroll.** Named in honor of former Seattle Mariner right fielder (and native of Japan) Ichiro Suzuki and served at Safeco Field, it's a spicy tuna sushi roll.

- **Pierogies.** Pittsburgh Pirates fans consider pierogies their signature food. They're a sort of ravioli stuffed with potatoes, cheese, and onions, and served topped with butter, salt, and black pepper.

- **Rocky Mountain Oysters.** They're not really oysters. They're calf testicles, halved, battered, and deep-fried. The only ballpark that has them is Coors Field in Denver.

- **Boiled Peanuts.** Turner Field in Atlanta serves them. Raw green peanuts are boiled in their shells in salty water for hours, until the shells turn soggy and a bit slimy. Fans rip off the shells and toss them on the ground. (Boiled peanuts are said to be an acquired taste.)

CHAPTER 6

SLIME AFTER SLIME

~ FUN FACT ~

THE GERMAN WORD FOR MUCUS
IS *NASENSCHLEIM* ("NOSE SLIME").

OOH, OOH THAT SMELL: Some people's feet sweat so much every day they could fill a pint jar with the stuff. And the sweatier the feet, the more they smell. The smell is actually caused by bacteria that lives on the skin. Its favorite food? Sweat. The bacteria eats the sweat and excretes waste that causes that stinky foot smell.

INSTA-QUIZ
Q: WHAT IS BLENNOPHOBIA?
A: THE FEAR OF SLIME.

A RARE TREAT: That red juice oozing from rare roast beef isn't blood. (That's *hemoglobin*, found in arteries.) Roast beef juice is caused when *myoglobin*, a purplish-colored protein found in the tissue of meat, combines with oxygen in the air to make bright red *oxymyoglobin*.

- **British Columbia:** Garbage collectors in the town of Oak Bay don't have to pick up trash if it "oozes."

- **Alaska:** An orange goo washed ashore near a remote village in 2011. It let off a gassy stink and worried locals could not identify it. The ooze turned out to be millions of microscopic eggs from some type of crustacean.

- **Miami:** In 2012, golden slime started oozing off walls in a couple's home. The cause? A swarm of 60,000 bees had built a hive in the walls. The golden "slime" was honey.

⤳ SHARE SOME WITH MOM!

Some acne creams and face creams share a common ingredient: snail slime. The slippery ooze has been found to reduce scarring caused by acne. Known scientifically as *glycoconjugate*, snail slime also smooths wrinkles around the eyes and forehead.

Joe Wad

You'll never see these words and phrases on a school spelling list. But you *can* build brain power if you memorize the words and their meanings. Use your slimy vocabulary to gross out your friends and impress your teachers (or vice versa).

★ ★ ★ ★

- **Eruck:** To belch.

- **Yackum:** Cow dung.

- **Gooey:** A gob of phlegm.

- **Joe-wad:** Toilet paper.

- **Gug:** An unpleasant person.

- **Dustman:** A corpse.

- **Alley apple:** Horse manure.

- **Drain the bilge:** To vomit.

- **Snow:** Underwear.

- **Grubber:** An unclean person.

- **Ubble-gubble:** Complete nonsense.

EAT SLUGS!

A record-breaking 50 banana slugs were eaten in 2002 during a slug-eating contest in California. Banana slugs are a bright yellow, slimy, shell-less mollusk  found on the floor of redwood forests. Banana slugs are great recyclers. They gobble up fallen leaves, mushrooms...even dead animals. So they play a vital role in building soil. Which makes us wonder, "Why eat them?"

> "I won't eat snails. I prefer fast food."—Strange de Jim

GOOSEBUMPS: Most mammals have hair to keep them warm. Humans used to be covered in the stuff. In cold weather, tiny muscles at the base of each hair constrict, causing the hairs to stand up. Air gets trapped between the hairs and creates a layer of insulation to warm the body. Without so much hair, that reaction gives people goosebumps.

(Caution! If you have a weak stomach, skip this list.)

- The average city water treatment plant processes enough human waste every day to fill 72 Olympic-sized swimming pools.

- A tapeworm can grow to a length of 30 feet inside human intestines. (That's about as long as a school bus.)

- According to a survey, more than 10% of Americans have picked someone else's nose.

- Tears are made up of almost the same ingredients as urine.

- Every day, most people fart enough to inflate a small balloon.

- The crusty goop you find in your eyes when you wake up is the exact same mucus you find in your nose—boogers.

- For those who haven't puked yet, here are eleven ways to say vomit: upchuck, hurl, barf, heave, Ralph, hug porcelain, yak, throw doughnuts, zuke, and blow chunks.

GROSS GAME AWARD: The Pressman Toy company was started in New York in 1922 by Jack Pressman. In 1995, the company came out with the Gooey Louie game. The game's goal? To pick green rubbery gooeys out of Louie's giant plastic nose. If a player picked the "wrong" gooey, Louie's brain and eyes would pop out. The talking version of the game has some great lines: "Pick me a winner!", "This is soooo gross!" and "This really tickles!" What do parents say about the game? "The boogers are a little sticky and tend to pick up dust, cat hairs and the like, but they can be easily rinsed off" and "It would be more fun if gummy worms were substituted for the boogers. Pull and eat!"

"People want to know why I write such gross stuff. I like to tell them I have the heart of a small boy... and I keep it in a jar on my desk."

—Stephen King

Step 1: Gather materials.   *Step 2: Begin the mutation.*

You'll need 1 teaspoon soluble psyllium fiber (the stuff that leads to smooth moves in the bathroom), 1 cup water, green food coloring, and acrylic glow paint.

Pour the water into a large microwave-safe bowl. Add the fiber and stir it up a bit to encourage the slime to mutate. It takes radioactive power to create glow-in-the-dark slime, so...

DEATH-DEALING SLIME ALERT: This glowing slime is for playing with, not eating. So DO NOT EAT the slime. It can swell in your throat and cause choking.

Step 3: Nuke the slime.   *Step 4: Add the glow.*

Microwave the slime on high power for 3 minutes. Stir the slime, then return it to the microwave. Nuke it for 3 more minutes. (For drier slime, add another minute or 2.)

Add a drop of green food coloring and a little glow paint. Mix together for a nice green glow. To keep your slime extra slimy, store in a sealed baggie. It should stay shriek-inducing for up to a week.

Toxic Travel

Bored with Disneyland and Harry Potter World?
Check out these world-famous hot spots.

HOT SPOT: Ranipet, India
TRAVEL TIP: Don't wade in the river.

Ranipet sits on the banks of the majestic Palar
River, but the town's biggest business is leather
tanning. Half the leather in all of Asia moves
through Ranipet's factories. What makes the river
so hot? *Hexavalent chromium* is a waste product
of the tanning industry. The cancer-causing
compound pollutes the water at the highest
levels on Earth. Local farmers say the water
"stings like insects" if it touches your skin.

HOT SPOT: The Irish Sea
TRAVEL TIP: Don't go fishing.

Since the 1950s, the Sellafield Nuclear Power Plant
on the coast of Cumbria, England has been

dumping radioactive waste into the Irish Sea. It's still at it, too—about two million gallons are dumped into the sea *every day*, turning the Irish Sea into "the most radioactive sea in the world." The fish contain dangerous levels of plutonium-239 and cesium-137, both of which can cause cancer.

HOT SPOT: Linfen, China
TRAVEL TIP: Try not to breathe deeply.

This city of four-million people is considered the birthplace of Chinese culture. It's also the heart of China's coal country and everything in the city is covered in black soot. How bad is it? In 2008, *Time* magazine name Linfen "The Most Polluted City in the World." If you go, tourism officials will give you a mask with the words "I Can Breathe" written on it. If you don't wear the mask? There are no guarantees.

~~~ FUN FACT ~~~

ONE IN SIX AMERICANS LIVES WITHIN A MILE OF A TOXIC WASTE SITE.

⟿ WHAT A GAS!

Volcanoes erupt, geysers gush, but fumaroles...they just pass gas. Fumaroles are Earth's steam vents. They're found near active volcanoes where fiery hot magma lies close to the surface. Hot magma boils away underground water and turns it into steam. That steam then gets released through fumaroles. And boy does it stink. Why? It's filled with sulfur gases, the kind that smell like rotten eggs.

ACID REFLUX: Mud pots form when fumaroles (see above) fill with surface water. Hydrogen sulfide (a.k.a. "sewer gas") bubbles up through the water and gets eaten by bacteria. The bacteria convert the hydrogen sulfide to sulfuric acid, an acid strong enough to dissolve rock. That turns the fumarole into a "pot" of mucky clay that boils, burps, and throws out lumps of mud. So don't get too close! Even when it hasn't turned to sulfuric acid, hydrogen sulfide can kill.

CHAPTER 7

THE GAMES BEGIN!

～ FUN FACT ～

IN THE U.S., WHAT SPORTING GOOD OUTSELLS BASEBALLS, BASKETBALLS, AND FOOTBALLS COMBINED? FRISBEES.

BLUE VS. GREEN: Chariot racing was huge during the Roman Empire—kind of like NASCAR races are today. The Hippodrome in Constantinople (now Istanbul, Turkey) was the place to see the races, and to be seen. It was the biggest racing stadium in the ancient world. Ten chariots could race down the U-shaped track at one time. And up to 60,000 roaring fans could pack the seats. The city was divided between fans of the Blue and the Green racing teams. Fights often broke out between sides. But in AD 532, rival fans joined forces. Emperor Justinian had ordered the execution of two chariot drivers: one from the Blue team and one from the Green team. He held the drivers responsible for deaths

in their races. (That's like a U.S. President ordering the execution of Jeff Gordon and Dale Earnhardt, Jr.). Yelling "Nika!" ("Conquer!"), the Blue and Green fans trashed the stadium, set fire to the city, and tried to kick the emperor out of the palace. By the time the riots ended, 30,000 people had been killed.

THE FLYING WALLENDAS: The famous "Flying Wallendas" tightwalking troupe started out in 1922 as the "Great Wallendas." Their most famous act was called "the pyramid," created by the group's founder, Mario Wallenda. Here's how it works: Two pairs of performers walk the wire. Each of them supports another acrobat standing on a pole. Those two acrobats carry another pole. The seventh person in the pyramid stands on a chair that is balanced on that pole. All seven are at the mercy of a single mistake. The act isn't foolproof (or fall-proof). During a performance in Akron, Ohio, in the 1940s, the wire slipped. Four troupe members toppled from the wire. Luckily, they were unhurt. A reporter who saw the accident was amazed. "The Wallendas fell so gracefully that it seemed as if they were flying," he wrote. The nickname stuck. From then on, the troupe was known as the Flying Wallendas.

~~~→ FUN FACT ←~~~

BRAZILIAN FANS ARE SO ROWDY THAT MANY OF THE COUNTRY'S SPORTS FIELDS ARE SURROUNDED BY MOATS.

THERE'S A RECORD FOR THAT?

Here are some of the weirdest world records...
on record.

- **Broom-Balancing.** Leo Bircher (Switzerland)
  holds the record for balancing a broom—on
  his nose—for a record time of two hours, one
  minute.

- **Prune-Eating**. In 1984, Alan Newbold (USA)
  ate 150 dried plums in 31 seconds. (No word on
  whether he set a bathroom record a few
  hours later.)

- **Extreme Hula-Hooping.** In 2000, Roman
  Schedler (Austria) hula-hooped for 71 seconds
  straight. That may not seem very long, but he
  did it with a 53-pound tractor tire.

- **Ear-Wiggling.** Not many people can wiggle their ears at all. Kitendra Kumar (India) wiggled his 147 times in one minute.

- **Drumming.** Tim Waterson (USA) is one of the world's fastest drummers. In January 2002, he set a speed record, playing 1,407 beats in one minute...with his feet.

- **Bean-Eating.** Kerry White (England) ate a world record 12,547 beans in a 24-hour period.

- **Nailing.** In October 1999, Chu-Tang-Cuong (Vietnam) drove 116 nails into a wooden board in just 11 minutes. The twist: He did it with his bare hand.

- **Cockroach-Eating.** In 2001, Ken Edwards (England) ate 36 cockroaches in one minute. But Travis Fessler (USA) has a more extreme record: He held 11 live cockroaches (each at least 2.5 inches long) for 10 seconds...in his mouth.

DON'T SHOOT THE PUPPY! Unlike most video games—where the object is to *do* something—the object of this 2006 game is to *not* do something. On one end of the screen is a huge gun. On the other is an animated puppy. If the player presses a key or moves the mouse even slightly, the cannon fires and blows off the puppy's head. Game over! But if the player can go ten seconds without lifting a finger, the puppy lives, and the game is won.

POO PARK: Bon Bon is a Danish company that makes candy with a silly toilet-humor theme. Its most popular product is something called "Dog Fart." Bon Bon Land is the fourth-largest amusement park in Denmark. The park takes all of Bon Bon's cartoon-animal mascots and turns them into rides and attractions. The signature ride is the Dog Fart roller coaster. The coaster winds around giant mounds of dog doo, pooping dogs, and giant speakers that play fart noises. Other attractions include a roller coaster through a sewer filled with (fake) feces and vomiting rats, and statues of cows and dogs lifting their legs.

GO HOT DOGS! Believe it or not, these are the names of real high-school sports teams.

- **Poca Dots** (Poca High School, West Virginia)
- **Hot Dogs** (Frankfort, Indiana)
- **Deaf Leopards** (Arkansas School for the Deaf)
- **Fightin' Planets** (Mars, Pennsylvania)
- **Pretzels** (New Berlin, Illinois)

~~~ FUN FACT ~~~

DURING THE 1930S, SPEED TYPING WAS A POPULAR COMPETITIVE "SPORT."

PLAYING CHICKEN: In 1985, fans of Japan's Hanshin Tigers won a championship. They celebrated by throwing a plastic statue of Colonel Sanders from a nearby KFC restaurant into the Dotonbori River. Hanshin hasn't won another championship since. Fans blame it on the angry spirit of the Colonel. They tried several times to find the statue in the murky river. Pieces of the statue were finally found in 2009. But the left hand is still missing, and the curse continues.

The 1982 men's college basketball championship game was a fight to the finish: Georgetown vs. North Carolina. Neither team could pull ahead by more than three points. With under a minute left to play, Georgetown was leading 62–61. That's when North Carolina freshman Michael Jordan hit a jump shot to make the score 63–62. Georgetown's Fred Brown quickly rebounded the ball and ran to the other end, where he confidently passed it to an open player, James Worthy. Only problem: Worthy played for North Carolina. Georgetown fouled Worthy to stop the clock, but he missed both foul shots. The clock ran out and North Carolina won the game.

~~~ FUN FACT ~~~

HENRY FORD GAVE HIS SON EDSEL HIS FIRST
FORD CAR...WHEN THE BOY WAS 8 YEARS OLD.
EDSEL DROVE HIMSELF TO 3RD GRADE.

NOT JUST MRS. ELASTIC MAN: Edith Clifford made her professional showbiz debut in 1899. She was 15 years old. A few years later, she joined the Barnum & Bailey Circus with her husband, "elastic man" Thomas Holmes. During her career, Edith swallowed seriously scary things such as razor blades, bayonets, saw blades, and scissors. And swords? She's said to have gulped down 24 at one time. She's known in sword-swallowing circles as "the Champion Sword Swallower of the World."

BOMBS AWAY: In October 2010, students at Westwood Middle School were practicing soccer. An airplane passed overhead and dropped two small objects on the field. As they watched, the plane circled and dropped a third object on the field before flying away. The students called police, who found toilet paper...three rolls of it. Police tracked down the pilot. He wasn't a toilet paper terrorist. He was a 60-year-old Westwood High football fan. He wanted to show his school spirit by dropping streamers on the field at the start of an upcoming football game. The toilet paper "attack" was a practice run.

Building a Better Squirt Gun

When Uncle John was a kid, he had squirt guns that shot 5 to 10 feet at most. Today, there are water toys that shoot 50 feet or more. Here's why.

BOY WONDER

Lonnie Johnson loved to tinker. As a kid, he used to take his brothers' and sisters' toys apart to see how they worked. By high school, he'd graduated to mixing rocket fuel in the family kitchen. One year he used scrap motors, jukebox parts, and an old butane tank to create a remote-controlled, programmable robot...which won first prize in the University of Alabama science fair. Not bad for a kid from the poor side of Mobile, Alabama.

UNDER PRESSURE

Johnson got an engineering degree from Tuskegee Institute. He went to work at the Jet Propulsion Laboratory in Pasadena, California, but he still spent his time tinkering. One evening in

1982, he was experimenting with using water instead of Freon as a refrigeration fluid. As he was shooting water through a high-pressure nozzle in the bathtub, he thought, "Wow! This would make a neat water pistol."

He built a prototype squirt gun out of PVC pipe, Plexiglas, and a plastic soda bottle. He approached several toy companies...but none of them thought a squirt gun with a 50-foot range would sell.

BLAST OFF

In March 1989, Johnson went to the International Toy Fair in New York and tried to sell his invention again. This time, the Larimi Corporation was interested. They arranged a meeting with Johnson at their headquarters in Philadelphia. When everyone was seated, Johnson opened his suitcase, whipped out a prototype, and shot a burst of water across the entire room. Larami bought the gun on the spot. Within a year, the "Super Soaker" was the bestselling squirt gun in history.

~~~> MEET BUG BOY

A "bug boy" is a rookie or apprentice jockey. The name comes from the asterisks (***), or "bugs," that appear next to a

rookie's name on racing forms. The more "bugs" beside a name, the less experience the jockey has.

SORRY, MOM!

What do Cleveland Indians pitcher Bob Feller and Minnesota Twins outfielder Denard Span have in common? They both hit their mothers in the stands with a foul ball. Feller hit his mom in 1939 (he broke her collarbone). Span hit his mom during a spring training game in 2010. Both moms made full recoveries.

CHAPTER 8

MAD SCIENCE

~~ FUN FACT ~~

EVERY YEAR, U.S. DOCTORS LEAVE SURGICAL TOOLS
INSIDE ABOUT 1,500 PATIENTS.

~~~ IT CAME FROM THE SLIME

For thousands of years, people believed that living things could grow out of nonliving things. The famous Greek thinker Aristotle believed that oysters grew out of slime and eels grew out of mud. It's called "spontaneous generation." And

it was treated as fact, even into modern times. Flemish chemist Jan Baptist Helmont lived in the 1600s. He was one of the most respected scientists of his day. And...he believed that you could create animals using simple recipes. His recipe for making mice? Put some wheat on a dirty cloth. Let it sit for 21 days and—*Voilà!*—mice. Scorpions? Put basil leaves between two bricks and leave them in the sun. In the mid-1800s, scientists finally realized that living things only came from other living things.

"The good thing about science is that it's true whether or not you believe in it."

—Neil deGrasse Tyson

CHICKENS PREFER BLONDES: In 2003, Swedish scientists scooped up an Ig Nobel Prize. That's an American version of the Nobel Prize, given out for research that *first* makes people laugh, and *then* makes them think. The prizes celebrate the unusual and honor the imaginative. What did the Swedish scientists do? They trained roosters and chickens to peck portraits to show which humans they preferred. The fowl favored hunky guys and longhaired ladies with bee-stung lips. "This suggests that man and chicken share similar wiring," said one of the study's authors.

MICKEY MOUSE IDEA: In January 2012, Japanese scientists announced that they had created a mouse that tweets like a bird. They had been cross-breeding mice and watching them for abnormalities. "We checked the newly born mice one by one," said researcher Arikuni Uchimura. "One day, we found a mouse that was singing like a bird." He added that he hoped his research would lead to the creation of a talking mouse. "I know it's a long shot," he said, "but I'm doing this with hopes of making a Mickey Mouse someday."

MAGIC? OR MAD SCIENCE

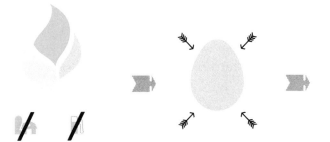

Step 1: Find an Adult Helper.   *Step 2: Gather Materials.*

1   **2**

Warning: This experiment uses fire. So don't do it in a barn full of hay. Or a gas station. Or, more importantly, without an adult present. (And don't be sneaky; the adult has to be *awake*.)

You'll need one peeled hard-boiled egg, an empty (and dry) glass fruit juice or tea bottle, a little vegetable oil, a 3-inch paper square, a match and a lighter.

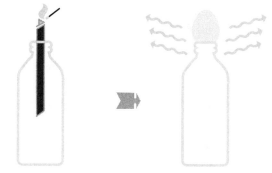

Step 3: Light a Fire.　　　　*Step 4: Watch in Amazement!*

Rub a little of the oil around the inside lip of the bottle. Fold the paper into a strip that can be easily dropped into the bottle. Light one end of the strip of paper and drop it into the bottle.

Set the egg on the opening of the bottle while the paper is still burning. The egg will start to wiggle, and then it will squeeze itself through the opening, falling into the bottle.

Death Ray

Scientist and inventor Nikola Tesla died in 1943 in a New York hotel suite. He left behind a mystery.

For 40 years before World War II, Nikola Tesla was one of the most famous scientists in the U.S. He was a genius inventor. But he had serious image problems. Most people thought he was nuts.

In 1934, Tesla claimed to have perfected a particle-beam ray. He said that his "death ray" could bring down enemy planes from 250 miles away or drop a million men dead in their tracks. The first Superman cartoon made fun of Tesla's claim. It featured a mad scientist (based on Tesla) terrorizing New York City with his death ray.

Was Tesla really mad? When he died, a little-known U.S. agency (the Alien Property Custodian office) hauled away truckloads of paper, furniture, and artifacts from his hotel room. Then they sealed everything away. No one knows what became of all that stuff. What is known? The FBI feared they'd find a working death ray among Tesla's things. They didn't. (Or so they say!)

Take Two Worms and Call Me in the Morning

Mother Nature can heal, if you're not afraid of her squirmy little helpers.

MAGGOT THERAPY

It sounds like something from a horror film—fat, cream-colored maggots eating their way through infected sores and wounds. It's not. It's medicine. Since ancient times, doctors have used maggots to prevent wounds from getting infected. In the 1940s, antibiotics replaced maggots. But bacteria adapted and started to become resistant to antibiotics.

Return of the Maggots: Maggots work by secreting digestive enzymes that feed on dead tissue. Those enzymes also kill bacteria in a wound and speed up healing. Doctors place between 200 to 300 maggots on a wound, then cover it—maggots and all—with mesh. Beneath the mesh, the maggots feed for 48 to 72 hours. When they're done, the doctors remove them. Wounds that haven't healed for months, even years, often respond quickly to maggot medicine.

LEECH THERAPY

Leeches are worms that live in fresh water and latch onto victims to suck up their blood. When these creatures bite, they secrete an anticoagulant called *hirudin* that prevents the victim's blood from clotting. That makes it easier for the leeches to feed. After being bitten by a leech, a person can bleed for hours.

For thousands of years, doctors used leeches on patients in a treatment called *bloodletting*. They thought bloodletting could cure everything from headaches to hemorrhoids. By the mid-1800s, it became clear that bloodletting didn't work, and leeches went down in history as a medical mistake. **Return of the Leeches:** In the 1980s, leeches made a comeback. Plastic surgeon Joseph Upton had reattached the severed ear of a five-year-old boy—an amazing medical feat at the time—but the tissues in the ear were dying. Upton rounded up some leeches, attached them to the boy's ear... and it healed.

Why? When a body part is reattached, blood may pool and clot, blocking circulation. Leeches suck up the extra blood, which prevents swelling. Their saliva releases chemicals that numb pain, fight infection, and calm inflammation. The fresh blood that flows to the damaged tissue helps it to heal and to produce new growth.

WHIPWORM THERAPY

Whipworms are a type of *helminth*—a worm classified as a parasite. Long, thin, and pale, whipworms thrive in places that lack proper sanitation. Their microscopic eggs are accidentally eaten, and then... they hatch. The newly-hatched worms migrate to the intestines, attach themselves to the walls, and chow down. Whipworms can cause everything from intense stomach distress to retardation in children.

In developed countries, better sanitation has largely wiped out whipworms.

Return of the Whipworm: Some doctors now believe it's possible for people to be *too* clean. (Huh?) Our immune systems are made to attack outside invaders like bacteria, germs, and parasites. But when invaders are in short supply, a person's immune system can misfire. The result: an autoimmune disease, which happens when the immune system attacks a person's own body instead of an invader.

"The most exciting phrase to hear in science? That's funny..."

—Isaac Asimov

People infected with whipworms rarely suffer from autoimmune diseases. Doctors wanted to see if patients' immune systems could be reeducated to attack whipworms and leave the body alone. Patients slurped down a dose of several hundred whipworm eggs in salty liquid and then let them grow. The little wrigglers did such a good job they may soon be available by prescription.

~~~ FUN FACT ~~~

HIPPOCRATES, THE "FATHER OF MEDICINE," PRESCRIBED
PIGEON POOP AS A CURE FOR BALDNESS.

HERE COMES PETER COTTONWOOD

In 2007, scientists at the University of Washington spliced a rabbit gene onto the DNA of a poplar tree—creating a "super poplar tree." The gene-altered tree can suck up toxins from contaminated soil. Any tree can safely absorb a few toxins, but the mutant trees can absorb hundreds, including cancer-causing pollutants such as benzene, vinyl chloride, and chloroform. And they do it up to 50 times faster. Opponents claim that the "mad scientists" are entering dangerous territory. Sharon Doty, one of the scientists, assures skeptics that a lot more research has to be done before these mutant trees make it out of the lab and into nature. "It's a beautiful thing that a rabbit gene is perfectly readable by a plant," she says. "I don't think it's something to fear."

CHAPTER 9

NERDS ARE US

41% OF AMERICANS SAY THEY'VE CONSIDERED ATTACKING
THEIR COMPUTERS. 7% HAVE DONE IT.

SUPER POWER: In 1982, a 10-year-old Italian boy named Benedetto Supino was reading a comic book in a dentist's office when it suddenly ignited. Another day, he awoke when his bed was on fire because his pajamas were burning. Soon after, his uncle decided to test his abilities. He handed Benedetto a plastic toy. Benedetto stared at it and the toy burst into flame.

JEDI ALERT: What was on board space shuttle *Discovery* when it blasted off in 2007? The lightsaber used by Mark Hamill as Luke Skywalker in *Return of the Jedi* (1983). The Jedi weapon headed into space to celebrate the 30th anniversary of the first Star Wars movie.

~~~ FUN FACT ~~~
SOME BATMAN COSTUMES HAVE A LABEL THAT READS,
"WARNING! CAPE DOES NOT ENABLE USERS TO FLY!"

THE TREK BEGINS: The original 1966 Star Trek TV series was a loser. (Sorry, Trekkies!) The show never climbed above 52nd place in the ratings. But, when the series was rebroadcast two years later, viewers became big fans. The world's first Trek Con took place in 1972 and 4,000 fans showed up (including sci-fi author Isaac Asimov, a huge fan). But the show's most popular character, Spock, was not there. Leonard Nimoy didn't want to be type cast. He even wrote a book called *I Am Not Spock*. But Spock fans would not be denied. In 1973, Nimoy appeared at Trek Con. Fans went crazy and he had to be ushered out by an army of security guards. Twenty years later Nimoy wrote another book: *I AM Spock*.

FIRST NERD: A Pulitzer Prize-winning author invented the word "nerd." He used it in a kids' book published in 1950: *If I Ran the Zoo*. "I'll sail to Ka-Troo. And bring back an It-Kutch, a Preep, and a Proo. A Nerkle, a Nerd, and a Seersucker, too." The author's name? Dr. Seuss.

WORMING IN: In 2003, a worm known as Blaster caused a crisis for software giant Microsoft. Once the worm got onto a computer, it messed with the operating system. A message appeared, counting down 60 seconds until the computer would shut down and restart. This on-and-off cycle would go on forever. And if a user shut down the computer manually, all data could be lost. Blaster's creator had a devious goal: to shut down Microsoft's Web site. Microsoft fought hard and blocked Blaster from its site. But before it was done, the worm had caused 500,000 computers to lose data. Despite a $500,00 reward, the identity of Blaster's creator remains a secret.

YOUR BRAIN USES 1/4 OF THE OXYGEN IN YOUR BLOOD.

Thomas Edison did *not* invent the first incandescent lightbulb. He *did* pioneer the use of carbonized cotton filaments—the kind that don't burn up when a light is switched on. On the other hand, Edison did invent a talking doll (1888) and a device for electrocuting cockroaches (1860s).

NAME THAT BUTTHEAD: In 1993, computer designers at Apple code-named a new computer model *Sagan*. This is usually considered an honor. "You pick a name of someone you respect," said an Apple employee. "And the code is only used while the computer is being developed." World-famous astronomer Carl Sagan asked that the code-name be changed. Apple agreed and changed the code-name to BHA, which stands for "Butt-head Astronomer." Sagan sued. And lost.

GENIUS SCHOOL: Believe it or not, there's a special school in New Jersey that has no classes, no tests, no degree programs, and...it's free. The catch? You have to be a genius to get in. The school was started in 1930 by noted educator Dr. Abraham Flexner. He wanted to give genius types a place to lose themselves in the world of ideas. A place where they would not have to worry about things like cooking or cleaning.

The school is called the Institute for Advanced Study, and it's located at 1 Einstein Drive in Princeton. At first, it was just a school for mathematics. Later other departments were added: Historical Studies, Natural Sciences, and Social Sciences. The geniuses invited to stretch their brains at IAS have included Albert Einstein, John von Neumann (Father of Game Theory), J. Robert Oppenheimer (Father of the Atomic Bomb), Kurt Gödel (called "the most important logician of our times"), and Heddy Goldman (archaeologist and the first female genius at IAS).

~~~ FUN FACT ~~~
MAY 25TH IS NERD PRIDE DAY

HOW TO WIN A NOBEL PRIZE

Step up all you brainiacs. Want to win the most respected prize on Earth? Here are the rules:

You can't nominate yourself. If you do, you'll be automatically disqualified. No exceptions!

You must be alive. Nominating dead people is not allowed. If you die, you're out of the running. Even if no one else was nominated.

There are no runners up. If you come in second to someone who drops dead before he or she picks up the medal, you still lose.

You can't win by default. If you come in second to someone who refuses the medal, do you win, or at least get the prize money? No and no.

No organizations allowed. With the exception of the Nobel Peace Prize, no single prize can be awarded to more than three people.

You don't get a laurel. The term "Nobel Laureate" is just an expression. If you win, you get a gold medal, a diploma with your name on it, and a cash prize (currently about $1 million). If you want to go around wearing a laurel-leaf crown like Julius Caesar, you'll have to make it yourself.

Unsung Superheroes

Imagine inventing America's most popular comic character...and getting paid only $130. That's what happened to these guys.

WHAT A CHARACTER!

One night in 1934, a 17-year-old guy who wanted to write comic books came up with the idea for a new character. The young man's name was Jerry Siegel and he was fresh out of high school. He was so excited about the idea that as soon as the sun came up, he ran twelve blocks to tell his friend and partner, Joe Shuster.

The pair started drawing up cartoon panels showing their hero in action. They sent samples to newspaper comic-strip editors all over the country. No one was interested. Four years later, DC Comics finally agreed to print one of Jerry and Joe's comics. DC paid the pair $130 for the 13-page story, and hired them as staff artists. Their new character made his first appearance in June, 1938. His name? Superman.

BILLION DOLLAR MAN

Superman was an instant smash. Over the years, he inspired a radio show, animated cartoons, a TV series, movies, and licensed products. In the 1970s alone, Superman products made $1 billion. But when Jerry and Joe signed on with DC as staff artists, they signed away all rights to Superman. From then on, all the money went to DC Comics.

"I had crushes on several girls. It occurred to me: What if I had something special going on for me, like jumping over buildings or throwing cars around. Then they would notice me."

—Jerry Siegel (explaining how he came up with the idea for Superman)

Jerry and Joe kept drawing the strip until 1948, when the company fired them. Why? They asked for a share of the profits. Both men sued DC Comics...and lost. By the 1970s, they were broke, living on money they made by selling old comic books and other memorabilia. In 1975, Warner Communications (owner of DC) decided to give Superman's creators pensions of $20,000 per year. (They upped it to $30,000 in 1981.) When the first Superman movie made $275 million, the company gave Superman's creators a bonus: $15,000 each. That's all the money Jerry and Joe ever got for their multi-billion dollar creation.

BORED TO DEATH

DC Comic's Superman was the nation's first superhero, but in the 1990s, comics changed. They featured tormented heroes who killed their foes in vengeful bloodbaths. Comic fans loved "the smart-alec snarls of Wolverine" and "the devilish depravity of Spawn." But Superman never killed his enemies. He preferred to turn them over to the proper authorities.

Fans found his patriotism and politeness boring. Superman's sales "plummeted faster than a speeding bullet." So DC Comics made plans to kill him. The impending death was nationwide news. Everyone wondered why kids were no longer interested in a "decent" hero. Comic stores played up the hype, flying flags with the Superman "S" dripping blood. Some stores even had the "Death" issue of Superman delivered in hearses.

NOT SO FAST!

Sales of Superman comics skyrocketed. Four months later, the superhero was back. It turned out that his dead body had been taken to a space-age "regeneration center," which brought him back to life. Buyers of the "Death" issue who thought they were getting a collector's item were outraged. Loyal fans resented DC's toying with them. But the stunt increased sales, leading DC's executive editor Mike Carlin to say that death was "good for Superman."

Spam I Am

It all started in 1970 with a comedy sketch on a
British TV show called *Monty Python's Flying
Circus*. In the sketch, a couple goes into a café.
The waitress offers them dish after dish, but
every dish has SPAM in it:

• Egg and SPAM

• Egg, bacon, and SPAM

• Egg, bacon, sausage, and SPAM

• Spam, egg, spam, spam, bacon and SPAM...

Finally, a horde of SPAM-loving Vikings storm
into the café and start singing: "Spam! Spam!
Spam! Spam! Lovely Spam! Lovely Spam!"
Users of a very early (and very slow) network
communication system called BITNET started
annoying each other by sending files containing
the words to the SPAM song. The term came to
mean any annoying use of the Internet.

SPAM! SPAM!

SPAM!

Yum!

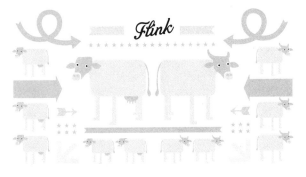

Flink

- **Yeevil:** a fork used for pitching manure.

- **Siffleuse:** a female wrestler.

- **Flink:** a group of 12 or more cows.

- **Zugzwang:** making a bad move in chess.

- **Alipile:** a person who removes armpit hair professionally.

- **Quodlibetarian:** Someone who argues about anything.

- **Ozostomia:** Evil-smelling breath.

- **Limophoitos:** Insanity caused by lack of food.

- **Ranarium:** A frog farm.

- **Wamfle:** To walk around with flapping clothes.

SMARTER THAN AVERAGE: Mensa International is the world-famous organization of "smart people." Anyone who passes their IQ test with a score in the upper 2% of the general population can join. There are about 100,000 members. Some may surprise you:

- Scott Adams (creator of the comic strip *Dilbert*)

- Geena Davis (Academy Award-winning actress)

- Norman Schwarzkopf (retired U.S. Army general)

- And 3-year-old Emmelyn Roettger, who can rattle off details about nebulas, black holes, and mitosis (cell division).

"The fact that some geniuses were laughed at does not imply that all who are laughed at are geniuses. They laughed at Columbus, they laughed at Fulton, they laughed at the Wright brothers. But they also laughed at Bozo the Clown."

—Carl Sagan

Leonardo: the Science Guy

While his countryman Christopher Columbus was out exploring the world, Leonardo da Vinci was exploring what made the world tick. He's been called the first modern scientist.

MIRROR, MIRROR

Leonardo was born in 1452 in the town of Vinci, Italy. He studied everything: anatomy (the body), botany (plants), physics, geology, meteorology (weather), aerodynamics (how things fly)—you name it. He filled notebooks with thoughts about everything he studied, and he added illustrations.

Those notes were a bit strange. Leonardo used "mirror writing"—he wrote backward. So to read his notes, you had to hold them up to a mirror. Why? The great thinker was very secretive. He didn't want anyone to steal his ideas. And, he didn't want just anyone to be able to read his notes. Leonardo had good reason to worry: While studying anatomy, he had dissected corpses.

When the Roman Catholic Church found out, church authorities stopped him. Cutting open bodies to study them went against the church's teachings. But before the church put a stop to his work, Leonardo had made progress: He had drawn the first accurate picture of the human heart.

I BELIEVE I CAN FLY!

Leonardo was curious about everything. And he had great intuition. He predicted the invention of the radio and the telephone. He came up with the idea after studying how water moves in waves.

> Leonardo's note to self: "Make glasses to magnify the Moon."

He decided that light and sound probably moved the same way, and he wrote this note: "Men from the most remote countries shall speak to one another and shall reply." Wireless telegraphy wasn't invented till 1899, making Leonardo about 400 years ahead of his time.

Leonardo was obsessed with the idea of human flight. He was the first person to study flight in a scientific way. But he got hung up on birds' wings. He spent years trying to invent a machine that would imitate the flapping wings of birds. Experts think that if he had worked on inventing a glider instead, he might have been the first person to fly.

Still, he was the first to think of a helicopter for human flight. He drew a design for what he called a "helix," a huge screw that would be launched by four men whirling the vertical shaft, each pushing on one of the horizontal spokes that projected from it. The design was correct in principal: The outer edge of the screw moved much faster than the central shaft, and this very rapid motion would compress the air below to lift the machine.

Then there was Leonardo's parachute—which he thought of as a means of transportation, not as a way to jump from an airplane. It was a tent 24 feet across and high. Leonardo tested it himself. How? He jumped off a tower.

PATRON SAINTS

In Leonardo's time, artists and inventors needed wealthy patrons to support their work. Among the devices Leonardo invented for his patrons were:
- a pump that raised water from a stream and ran it through a duke's castle,
- a heating system to warm a duchess's bath,
- floats for walking on water,
- an armored tank that looked like a flying saucer and could move (and fire guns) in any direction,
- a gadget for lighting cannons that worked and looked like a cigarette lighter, and
- stink bombs mounted on arrows.

"The human foot is a masterpiece of engineering and a work of art."
—Leonardo da Vinci

~~~ FUN FACT ~~~

IN 1994, BILL GATES PAID MORE THAN $30 MILLION FOR ONE OF LEONARDO'S NOTEBOOKS: THE CODEX LEICESTER.

SURF AND STREAM: In 2003, Microsoft's U.K. office was hard at work on a new product: the iLoo. (Loo is slang for "toilet" in Britain.) The iLoo would be a toilet with a built-in computer, complete with wireless keyboard and monitor. Users would be able to surf the Web while doing their business. Don't expect to be using one soon. When Microsoft bigwigs heard about the Web-surfing toilets, they canceled the program.

"I'm not a nerd, Bart. Nerds are smart."—Milhouse (*The Simpons*)

EINSTEIN'S BRAIN: In 1896, Einstein was a Ph.D. candidate and star student at a Swiss university with top grades in physics and math. Later, Einstein worked on a famous theory of relativity and banked the money for the Nobel Prize for Physics. But we're not talking about the fuzzy-haired genius, Albert. We're talking about his first wife, Maric. Some believe that Maric Einstein was the brains behind the world's most famous genius. Albert bragged that his wife was not only a great cook, she did his math calculations.

CHAPTER 10

SCHOOL
DAZE

〜〜 **FUN FACT** 〜〜

24 HOURS FROM NOW, YOU'LL HAVE FORGOTTEN
80% OF EVERYTHING YOU LEARNED TODAY.

SLOW LEARNERS: President Andrew Johnson didn't learn to write until he was 17. President Andrew *Jackson* wasn't sure if the Earth was round or flat. President Woodrow Wilson couldn't read until he was 11 years old. But... President Thomas Jefferson could read in seven

different languages and President Jimmy Carter could speed read—2,000 words per minute. (The average reader can read 275 words per minute.)

WHO FARTED?

A Museum in England had an exhibit called "The Roman Experience." Visitors could stroll through streets made to look just as they did in Roman times, including...real-life smells. The staff added a special odor called "flatulence" to the Roman latrines (old-style toilets). Unfortunately—the smell was *so* real several schoolkids vomited. "It is nice to see that the smell is so realistic," said the museum's director.

REAL NOTES TO TEACHERS

- "Dear School: Please excuse John being absent on Jan. 28, 29, 20, 31, 32, and also 33."

- "Sally won't be in school a week from Friday. We have to attend her funeral."

- "Please excuse Ray Friday from school. He has very loose vowels."

- "Please excuse Harriet for missing school yesterday. We forgot to get the Sunday paper off the porch, and when we found it on Monday, we thought it was Sunday."

- "Please excuse Mary for being absent. She was sick and I had her shot."

~~~ FUN FACT ~~~

YOU HAVE TO BE A HIGH SCHOOL GRADUATE TO PLAY FOR A BIG-LEAGUE BASEBALL TEAM

BIG BAD BULLY

In the early 1900s, an Italian boy named Benito
Mussolini was expelled from school for stabbing
another kid in the butt. He grew up to be...a
dictator. Mussolini supported Hitler during World
War II. Bad idea. His country was invaded, and
then torn apart by civil war. The Italians did more
than expel Mussolini. On April 28, 1945, they had
him executed by a firing squad.

~~~ FUN FACT ~~~

THE CHICAGO PUBLIC-SCHOOL SYSTEM REQUIRES BLIND
STUDENTS TO TAKE DRIVER'S EDUCATION CLASSES.

FORMER TEACHERS

- Horror writer Stephen King was once a high-school English teacher.

- Gene Simmons of 1970s American rock band *KISS* was once an elementary school teacher.

- Republican Senator Pete Domenici of New Mexico was a high-school math teacher.

- When Mr. T wasn't acting in *Rocky III* or TV's *The "A" Team*, he was teaching gym classes in Chicago. Pity the fools who got out of line!

- Famous poet Robert Frost worked as a teacher, a reporter, and a chicken farmer.

- Actor Jon Hamm of TV's *Mad Men* was a drama teacher at the high school he'd once attended.

- Before hitting it big, singer Sheryl Crow taught music at Kellison Elementary School in Missouri.

- Comedian Billy Crystal taught "everything from English to auto shop."

- While writing the first Harry Potter book, author J.K. Rowling taught English classes in Portugal.

TEACHERS' PETS

- A schoolteacher in Kansas brought his pet python to class to show students how to feed it. He was ordered to "cease and desist." Why? He wanted to feed puppies to the snake.

- A teacher in Georgia took her class to a nearby park—where they stole a duck from the pond. They took the duck back to school, where they planned to release it as a prank. The 23-year-old teacher was charged with "contributing to the delinquency of minors."

"Never let your schooling interfere with your education."

—Mark Twain

LET THE SUNSHINE IN: Researchers in California studied 21,000 students in California and Washington. They found that kids do better in school when they work in natural light than in artificial light. On tests, the kids scored up to 26% higher in reading and up to 20% higher on math.

SCHOOL'S OUT FOREVER!

Uncle John says, "Stay in school!" even though these billionaire drop-outs did not.

Sir Richard Branson. The founder of Virgin Records and Virgin Atlantic Airways was miserable at school. Why? He's dyslexic. Branson became a business entrepreneur at age 12. He left school at 17. His headmaster predicted he would "either go to prison or become a millionaire." He hasn't been sent to jail yet.

Walt Disney. As a schoolkid, Walt was a lot more interested in art than the Three R's. At age 16, he left school to try to enlist in the army. The army wouldn't take him. He was too young. As an adult, Disney became famous for Mickey Mouse and movies and theme parks. When he 58 years old, his high school gave him an honorary diploma.

 LOONEY LAWS: In Atlanta, Georgia, it's illegal to make faces at school kids while they're studying. In Binghamton, New York, ninth-grade boys are not allowed to grow mustaches.

Painful Lesson

If your teacher brings a dead animal for show-and-tell, you might want to flee while you can.

One morning in 2003, a Massachusetts high school teacher was driving his pickup truck to work. He saw a dead coyote in the middle of the road. So... he tossed it into the back of the truck and took it to school.

Later that day, Dowling showed his students how to skin an animal. He even let some of them touch the dead coyote. When school administrators heard, they shared a few more lessons with his students:

1. Touching dead animals can lead to rabies;
2. If an animal has been dead for awhile (like a road-killed coyote), there's no way to tell if it *has* rabies; and
3. Rabies can kill you if left untreated.

Every kid who touched the coyote had to get really painful rabies shots. And the teacher? He was suspended without pay.

THERE'S A SCHOOL FOR THAT?

- Roman gladiators went to gladiator school. The "school" was really a prison, with plenty of time for learning how to kill using weapons like spears, chains, swords, and lassos.

- The first Santa Claus School opened in September 1937 in Albion, New York.

- Teachers at the Clown School of San Francisco believe that inside of every person lives a ridiculous character just "dying" to get out.

- Oregon School of Tattoo Arts is run by a second-generation tattoo artist. The school trains students to become licensed tattoo artists.

- Sewer School grads learn to reach into a sludge pump to clean out everything that's been flushed in the night before, and "be proud of it."

CHAPTER 11

DUMB & DUMBER-ER

~~ FUN FACT ~~

TOUGH, BUT DUMB: SOUTH AFRICAN GIANT
BULLFROGS SOMETIMES ATTACK LIONS.

DUMB CROOK

In March 2011, Kevon Whitfield, 19, and a 14-year-old friend phoned Topper's Pizza in Clifton, Ohio, and ordered a pizza. What they really wanted to do was to rob the pizza delivery person. How do we know this? Because after Whitfield phoned in the order, he forgot to end the call. His cell phone was still connected to Topper's Pizza as he and his accomplice planned the robbery. A Topper's Pizza employee heard everything and called the cops. The police replaced the delivery driver with an undercover officer. He arrested the two crooks as they tried to pull the heist.

FUN FACT

THE FIRST GOTHAM CITY WASN'T IN BATMAN COMICS. THE ORIGINAL GOTHAM CITY WAS A MYTHICAL ENGLISH TOWN WHOSE RESIDENTS WERE EXTREMELY STUPID.

DUMBER CROOK: In August 2010, Shane Alexander, 20, and Jason Vantress, 30, went to an Oregon supermarket. They started cutting the tags off items and stuffing the goods into their backpacks. They took clothes, shoes, tools—even a couple of blenders. A clerk saw what they were doing and quickly notified police. It wasn't very difficult: there were 60 uniformed officers already in the store. Turns out it was "Shop with a Cop" day, an annual event during which officers assist underprivileged kids with back-to-school shopping. Alexander and Vantress were arrested seconds later. "Crooks think they're smarter than the average bear," said Officer Pete Simpson. "And they're not."

DUMB SCIENCE: In 2009, British scientists gave a group of ducks access to a pond, a water trough, and a shower. Why? So they could find out if ducks like standing in the rain. After three years watching the ducks, the scientists had an answer: Ducks like standing under a shower better than standing in still water. The duck study cost more than half a million dollars.

CRAIGSLIST DUMB POST AWARDS

Just because you *can* post it on Craigslist, doesn't mean you should. (Yes...these are real posts.)

- "Free toilet. Could be fixed up. A little dirty, and it leaked and overflowed last time it was used. My son stuffed an action figure down it. So if anyone picks this up and fixes it, can you drop the action figure back off at my house?"

- "I have a bedroom available for a male or female roommate. The apartment is spacious and well lit. I work as a researcher and I'm also pursuing a Master's Degree. One more thing. On our bathroom door is a checklist. I like to keep a record of my bowel movements and I expect you to do the same."

- "I have some banana slugs. I will lease them out for $1 per day. You just come and catch them, and keep sliding dollar bills under my front door. I am trying to save up for a flat screen TV."

- "I found four cockroaches in a box of Triscuits a few months back. I hate to have to get rid of them but I'm moving to a smaller place and won't really have the room for them anymore. Re-homing fee of $15 each or $50 for all four."

- "Looking for an assistant to help with texting—replies, deleting texts, reading texts, and filtering texts. I get 40–50 texts an hour. This is a full-time position and you must be wherever I am, because my phone is always with me."

- "I need someone to hide Easter eggs in my apartment when I am not there. They are small and filled with candy."

DUMB CANDLE

White Castle fast-food chain is best known for its onion-flavored mini-burgers called "sliders." In 2010, the chain began selling a scented candle. It comes in a cardboard sleeve that looks like a White Castle burger package. And it smells like steamed burgers and grilled onions. The first 10,000 candles sold out in 48 hours.

DUMBER CANDLE: Sniff Candles offers a line of scented candles for...dogs. (We're not kidding!) Scents include "Fart and Away," "Day in the Hamptons," and "Splendor in the Grass." Each candle costs $28. Why so pricey? They don't just give off smells that dogs like. They're specially made "for the health and well-being of your best friend." They're also 100%-organic with "the perfect blend of essential oils to offer emotional balance and energy." Not so dumb: a portion of each sale supports animal rescue and gives back to the "dog community."

DUMB WEAPON: In September 2009, sunbathers at Madeira Beach, Florida, saw Keith Marriott, 41, struggling in the surf. When they ran into the water to save him, he jumped up and started throwing jellyfish at them. Witnesses said he repeated the stunt several times. Each time he threw jellyfish at people who ran to help him. He was arrested.

DUMBER WEAPON: William Singalargh, age 27, of New Zealand was arrested after getting into a fight with a 15-year-old boy. During the brawl, Singalargh grabbed a hedgehog (no word on where he got it) and threw it at the kid. The prickly porcupine-like creature hit the boy's leg. It caused several punctures and severe swelling. Singalargh was fined $500 for simple assault. (The original charge of assault with a deadly weapon was dropped because the hedgehog was "not deadly enough.")

~~~ FUN FACT ~~~

ACCORDING TO DOG BREEDERS, AFGHAN HOUNDS ARE THE DUMBEST DOGS.

Young Marines Make
Tasty Christmas Treats

TREES CAN BREAK WIND

MOST DOCTORS AGREE
THAT BREATHING REGULARLY
IS GOOD FOR YOU

PARENTS KEEP KIDS HOME
TO PROTEST SCHOOL CLOSURE

STUDENTS COOK & SERVE GRANDPARENTS

YELLOW SNOW STUDIED
TO TEST NUTRITION

The South Orange school district in New Jersey suspended a sixth grader for three weeks. Why? The student threatened a teacher with...a package of Nutter Butter cookies. The teacher had a severe nut allergy, and the student in question had an unopened pack of cookies in class. Seems the student had joked with classmates about rubbing a Nutter Butter cookie on the teacher.

DUMBER AT SCHOOL: In 2007, Shelby Sendelbach, a sixth-grader at Mayde Creek Junior High in Katy, Texas, confessed to writing "I love Alex" on the wall of the school gym. Shelby was called to the principal's office, questioned by a police officer, read her rights, and charged with a "level 4 infraction"—the same level applied for gun possession and making terrorist threats. And she was sent to a special "disciplinary" school for four months. Officials said they were just following the rules.

Fabulous Flops

Some products, like the Ford Model T and the Sony Walkman, change the world. Others are so dumb they fail, and give us something to laugh at.

Thirsty Dog! Soda. In 1994, the Original Pet Drink Company created a soft drink for dogs. It was "crispy beef" flavored and sweetened with fructose and glucose. Original Pet pitched Thirsty Dog! as better for your dog than water. At 200 calories per bottle, the sugary soda made one of the most common pet health problems— obesity—even worse. And compared to $1.79 a liter, drinking out of the toilet was a lot cheaper.

Grubbies Sneakers. Ever heard of pre-washed jeans? In 1966, B.F. Goodrich came up with a similar idea: "pre-tattered" sneakers. You didn't have to wait months for your sneakers to look beat-up. With Grubbies, all you added was the foot odor.

Plastic Snow. Before snowmaking machines, ski resorts needed a way to keep people skiing during dry spells. In the mid-'60s, plastic seemed like the answer. One resort spread tons of Styrofoam pellets on their ski runs. The pellets quickly blew away. Another company offered mats with nylon bristles, like Astroturf. New Jersey's Great Gorge ski area laid them out on its slopes. They worked well...unless you fell down. "The bristles were needle-sharp and everybody tore his pants," founder Jack Kurlander told reporters. "There was blood, blood, blood. Boy were we embarrassed!"

Pea Fries. Kids love French fries, right? Right! So in the 1970s, American Kitchen Foods introduced a new frozen food: "I Hate Peas!" The package label described the food as "the new way to get vegetable goodness." What was in the package? Peas...mashed into a paste, and then shaped to look like French fries. As one kid said, "They might look like fries, but they still taste disgusting." Other vegetables in the "I Hate" line: corn, carrots, green beans, spinach, and beets. Kids hated those, too.

⟡ GAME SHOW GOOFS

Being on a game show may look easy, but under those hot television lights, contestants' mouths sometimes disconnect from their brains.

Game Show: *The Weakest Link*

Host: "What insect is commonly found hovering above lakes?"

Contestant: "Crocodiles."

Game Show: *Family Feud*

Host: "Name something a blind man might use."

Contestant: "A sword."

Game Show: *Go*

Host: "What moos?"

Contestant: "A car."

Game Show: *Steve Wright Radio Show*

Host: "What is the capital of Australia? And it's not Sydney."

Contestant: "Sydney."

CHAPTER 12

BEYOND TOP SECRET

~~~ FUN FACT ~~~

SHH! THE FORMULA FOR PLAY-DOH IS TOP SECRET—
PLAYSKOOL KEEPS IT UNDER LOCK AND KEY.

FOUND ON EBAY: In September 2008, an English postal worker bought a digital camera on eBay for about $30. After he'd used it a few times, he looked through the camera's memory. Along with his vacation pictures, he found photos of terrorists, missiles, rockets, and fingerprints. He also found snapshots of documents detailing a spy computer system that could have been used to hack into the network. The postal worker contacted the British government. After he was interrogated for a few hours, he was told that he'd accidentally been sold a camera that had been used by an MI6 agent (the spy's name was never released).

⟿ SECRET INGREDIENT
Burger King's Fat Free Ranch Dressing and Wendy's Low Fat Honey Mustard Dressing both have a secret ingredient to make them look creamy. What is it? *Titanium dioxide,* which is also found in...sunscreen. (Yum!)

FURRY SPY: In 1999, a furry toy with googly-eyes and big pink ears made it onto U.S. spy agencies' lists of possible double agents. Its name: Furby. The toy's embedded computer chip could record up to 200 words. And it could repeat what it recorded.

A toy like that could spill a lot of secrets. The National Security Administration came up with a solution: ban the Furby! The chatty toy was no longer allowed in agency offices.

FAMOUS AND BROKE: Most people have heard of Eliot Ness. He was the government agent who put gangster Al Capone in prison in 1931. Ness was just 27 years old when he became famous for that feat. Then things went sour for the G-Man. His wife left him. He started a couple of businesses that failed. He even got fired from an alarm company. In 1947, Ness ran for mayor of Cleveland. He lost. And, he ended up with so much debt he had to file for bankruptcy. Ness died of a heart attack in 1957.

SECRET AGENCIES: REVEALED

- **The KGB** was the notorious Soviet spy agency during the Cold War era. KGB stands for *Komitet Gosudarstvennoy Bezopasnosti*. Translation: "Federal Security Service." As the secret international arm of the Soviet Union, the agency stopped anti-Communist revolutions in Hungary (1956) and Czechoslovakia (1968). But KGB agents tried—and failed—to assassinate American actor John Wayne in 1949.

- **The Stasi** was East Germany's secret police *and* its intelligence agency between the 1950s and the 1980s. (Sort of like a combination of the C.I.A. and the F.B.I.) Stasi is short for *Staatssicherheit*, or "state security." Stasi agents, many of whom were former Nazi officers, worked with the KGB to spread and enforce Communist rule in Eastern Europe. The agency funded terrorist groups in West Germany, seeking to bring that country down. By the late 1980s, 2% of all East Germans either worked for the agency or were unpaid informants.

- **Mossad** is the state intelligence agency of Israel. Its full name? *Ha Mossad le Moudiin ule Tafkidim Meyuhadim* (Hebrew for "The Institute for Intelligence and Special Tasks"). Its most famous act: locating and executing members of Black September, a Palestinian terrorist group who murdered 11 Israeli athletes at the 1972 Summer Olympics in Munich, Germany.

~~~ FUN FACT ~~~

THE CLOWNS WHO PORTRAY RONALD MCDONALD ARE
FORBIDDEN TO REVEAL THEIR TRUE IDENTITIES.

Splashdown! ⬤➡

In case an evil genius sneaks up behind you
when you're standing on a bridge and pushes
you off, here's what you need to know to survive.

1. Aim for the deepest water—you'll be
   traveling so fast that even if you survive the
   impact with the water, you could be injured
   or killed by slamming into a shallow bottom.

2. While you're in the air, keep your body as
   straight as possible. Point your toes down
   (guys, protect your crotch with your hands).
   Also, clench your buttocks to keep water from
   rushing in and causing internal damage.

3. Once you're in the water, fan out your arms
   and legs to slow your descent.

4. In case the evil genius tosses other people or
   objects down behind you, swim away as
   quickly as you can. (And call the cops!)

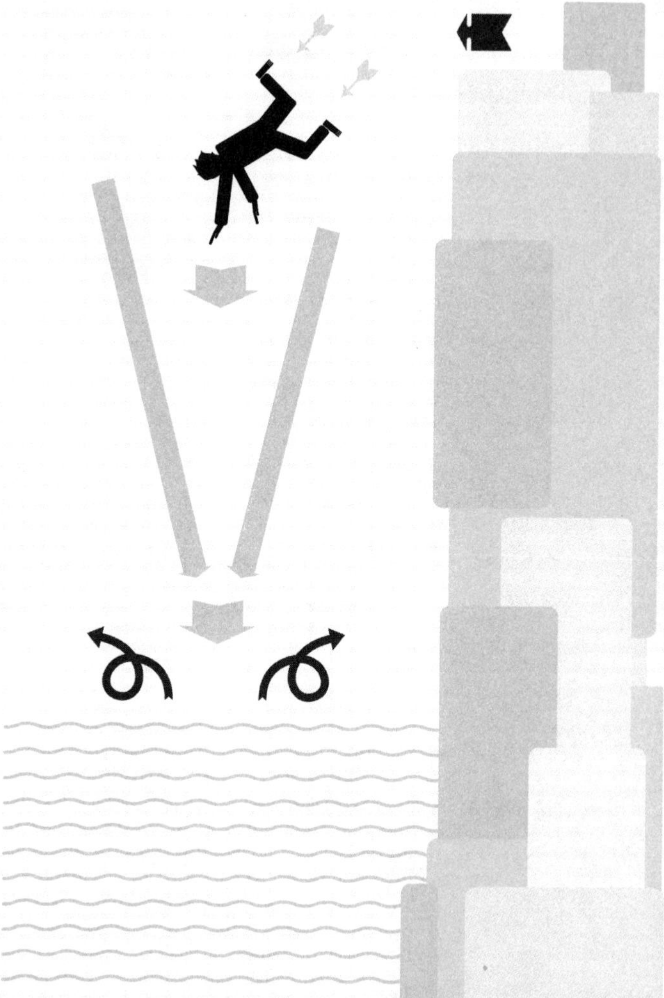

6 WAYS TO CATCH A SPY IN A LIE

1. Watch for sweating and squirming.

2. Notice if the person crosses his arms or sits behind a desk to create a "barrier" between you.

3. Watch the eyes. Liars blink more, and when they smile, their eyes aren't smiling, too.

4. Ask for details. A lie will often fall apart if you ask for more information.

5. Listen for inconsistencies.

6. Listen for giveaways. Someone who's lying may complain, be less friendly, or say things such as "to be honest."

"Ben Franklin put it well—
'A secret known to three people
can be kept, as long as two of
them are dead.'"

—Arthur C. Clarke

~ FUN FACT ~

IN JAPAN, THE JAMES BOND FILM *DR. NO* WAS ORIGINALLY
TRANSLATED AS *WE DON'T WANT A DOCTOR*.

SKULL & BONES:

This secret society was
founded at Yale University
in 1833. Only 15 senior-year
students get in each year.
Members meet twice a week
in a grim, windowless
building called the Tombs.

Unlike most college fraternities, Skull & Bones
has one main goal: to put its members into places
of power after college. Of course, no outsider
really knows for sure. Members are sworn to
secrecy for life. Past members include three U.S.
Presidents (both George Bushes and William
Howard Taft) as well as the descendants of such
famous American families as the Pillsburys,
Weyerhausers, Rockefellers, Vanderbilts, and
Whitneys. Some say the Order (as it's called by
members) works to create a world controlled and
ruled by the elite—members of Skull & Bones.

REAL TOYS OF THE CIA

Uncle John loves those clever spy gadgets in James Bond movies. As it turns out, some of them are real. Here are a few actual spy tools.

IT LOOKS LIKE: A pencil
BUT IT'S REALLY: A .22-caliber pistol
DESCRIPTION: This camouflaged .22 comes preloaded with a single shot. To fire, just turn the pencil's eraser counterclockwise and squeeze. The pencil-gun has a firing distance of up to 30 feet.

IT LOOKS LIKE: A belt buckle
BUT IT'S REALLY: A hacksaw
DESCRIPTION: Fitted inside a hollow belt buckle is a miniature hacksaw. When the buckle is opened, a small amount of pressure is released from the saw's frame, exerting tension on the blade. This makes the saw a more efficient cutting tool for sawing through, for example, handcuffs. The belt-buckle saw will cut through

anything from steel to concrete in about 15 minutes. It will also rip through rope and nylon. Don't wear belts? Buckles can be put on coats and luggage, too.

IT LOOKS LIKE: Eyeglasses
BUT IT'S REALLY: A dagger
DESCRIPTION: Concealed in the temple arms of these CIA glasses are two sharp blades. Disguised as the reinforcing wire found in most eyeglass frames, the daggers are designed to be used once and broken off at the hilt, inside the victim. The lenses are cutting tools, too. The lower edges are ground to razor sharpness and can be removed by heating or breaking the frames.

IT LOOKS LIKE: A felt-tip marker
BUT IT'S REALLY: A blister-causing weapon
DESCRIPTION: Don't mistake this pen for your Sharpie, and be careful: You wouldn't want it leaking in your pocket. A little over three inches long, the marker distributes an ointment that creates blisters on the skin. To activate the weapon, press the marker's tip down on a surface for one minute—then simply apply a thin coating of the

colorless oil over any area, such as a keyboard or door handle. The ointment will penetrate clothing and even shoes. And it will cause temporary blindness if it comes in contact with the eyes. Blisters will cover the skin wherever contact is made within 24 hours and last for about a week.

IT LOOKS LIKE: False teeth

BUT IT'S REALLY: A concealment device (and much more)

DESCRIPTION: What could possibly fit inside dentures? A lot more than you'd think. A cutting wire or a compass can be placed in a small tube and hidden under a false tooth. A rubber-coated poison pill can be carried the same way. The

poison can be swallowed (to avoid capture) or poured into an enemy's food as a weapon. And if that's not enough, a spy can whip out the dental plate and use its sharp scalloped edge for digging, cutting, or even hand-to-hand combat.

⟿ EYE SPY A SPY

- Before founding the Boy Scouts, Robert Baden-Powell had been a spy in South Africa.

- She's a world-famous chef, but during World War II, Julia Child worked for a U.S. spy agency and operated out of Sri Lanka.

- Film star Jackie Chan's father was a spy for Taiwan.

- The character of James Bond is based on William Stephenson, a real-life spy from Winnipeg.

- After retiring from baseball in 1939, catcher Moe Berg was a spy for the U.S. in World War II.

- Before he became President of the United States (1989–1993), George H. W. Bush was the director of the country's biggest spy agency: the C.I.A.

"More history is made by secret handshakes than by battles."
—John Barth

- **Terminated with extreme prejudice:** When a spy agency executes one of its own spies for betraying the agency.

- **Fumigating:** Searching a home or office to remove any listening devices, or "bugs."

- **Spy dust:** Invisible powder the KGB sprinkled on door knobs, inside cars, etc., so they could track diplomats and suspected spies as they moved around Moscow.

- **Smudger:** A photographer.

- **Jack in the box:** A fake torso, sometimes inflatable, that's put in a car to fool surveillance teams about how many people are riding in it.

- **Shopworn goods:** Spy information so old or out of date that it's completely useless.

- **Backstopping:** Creating fake background material (employers, phone numbers, etc.) to enhance the credibility of a spy's cover.

- **The Farm:** Camp Peary, the 10,000-acre facility near Williamsburg, Virginia, where CIA agents get their spy training.

ARTSY-FARTSY

MY PET HUMAN: In 2004, an artist named David Blandy put an message on his website: *The 18th-century tradition of housing a human pet at the bottom of your garden to impress the neighbours is set to return. I will seal myself off from the outside world and reside in a house with similar proportions to a rabbit hutch.* His goal was to show that in today's world, people care more about their electronic gadgets than each other. So how long did the experiment last? A few weeks.

HOLLYWOOD PETS

Actor Nicholas Cage has owned some weird pets: an octopus, a shark, a crocodile, and two king cobras. Director Frank Capra had a pet raven named Jimmy and found a place for him in his movies. In the Christmas classic, *It's a Wonderful Life* (1946), Jimmy the raven sits on Uncle Billy's desk in the Bailey Building and Loan. Before he played *Star Trek*'s Mr. Spock, actor Leonard Nimoy owned a pet store.

CANDY-MAKING SQUIRRELS: The movie *Charlie and the Chocolate Factory* (2005) faithfully adapted the famous "nut scene" from Roald Dahl's original book. The scene shows a room full of squirrels who crack nuts and sort them on a conveyor belt. Fantasy right? What viewers might not know is that those big screen squirrels are *real*, not animated. Director Tim Burton found them at a "school for squirrels." At the squirrel school, 200 of the rodents spent 19 weeks learning to sit on stools, and to crack and sort nuts—just for that short scene.

AY, CHIHUAHUA! The most famous fast-food character of the 1990s was invented by chance. Two advertising execs, Chuck Bennett and Clay Williams, were eating lunch at a grill in Venice, California. "We saw a little Chihuahua run by that appeared to be on a mission," Bennett says. "We looked at each other and said, 'That would be funny.'" The men went on to make Gidget—the Taco Bell Chihuahua—an international superstar. Gidget died in 2009 at the age of 15 (about age 76 in human years).

MR. HAND-FART MAN

Are you one of those talented kids who can make "farting" noises by squeezing your palms together? If not, maybe you should be. "Manualism," or hand music, has probably been around since some prehistoric person accidentally made a fart noise with his hands. But the first known mention of it was in 1933. A Michigan farmer named Cecil Dill appeared in a Universal Newsreel clip playing hand music. He claimed to have discovered the sound when he was a boy. He was rubbing his hands together one cold day and "Phttt!!!" After that, he practiced hand-farts until he could play the song "Yankee Doodle." In the news clip he plays—with his hands—"Let Me Call You Sweetheart." And it's actually good.

~~~ TOOTHY SWEETHEARTS

In 2006, scientists at the Blackpool Sea Life Centre in England had a problem. They wanted two of their sharks, Bloodnose (a male) and Lucky (a female), to mate. The sharks weren't in the mood. The scientists tried piping music through speakers above the sharks' tank. Classical music by Mozart and Beethoven didn't work. Neither did an opera by Puccini or pop songs by Barry White. What did? "My Heart Will Go On," the love song from the movie *Titanic*, sung by Celine Dion.

WACKY MUSICIAN: German composer Ludwig van Beethoven lived from 1770–1827. His *Ninth Symphony* is one of the greatest pieces of classical music ever written. But the brilliant composer was a little...odd. He never washed his clothes. He counted out exactly 60 beans for each cup of coffee. And he once returned to a ballroom still buttoning up his trousers after a bathroom break.

IT'S COMING RIGHT AT YOU!

How do 3D movies make objects pop out of the screen and head right for the audience? Uncle John lets the secrets of 3D out of the projection booth and zaps them directly into...your brain!

HEY, TWO EYES!

It takes just two things to see: an eye and a brain. Light enters the eyeball through the cornea. It's focused and then sprayed onto the retina. The retina converts the light into signals that are sent to the brain along the optic nerve. Then the brain processes the information and figures out what you're seeing. (Oh! Hi, Mom!)

All of this would work even if you only had one eye. With that extra eye, you get a special gift: stereo vision. That lets you gauge, with a fair deal of accuracy, the distance of objects in front of you. This happens because your two eyes are set slightly apart (two inches is the norm). So even though both eyes are looking at the same scene, each has a different take on whatever it is you're looking at (one a little more to the left, and the other a little more to the right).

THE MOVING FINGER

Both eyes send the information to the brain's visual centers. The brain fuses the two pictures together, and you "see" one picture that incorporates those two different perspectives and provides you with depth perception. The melding is so seamless you don't even notice that you're really seeing two views of the same scene. Try this: Hold up one finger. Keep both eyes on the finger as you slowly move it toward the bridge of your nose. As it moves closer, you'll see two images of your finger appear. Why? Because your eyes' separate fields of vision don't overlap there.

BUILT-IN BINOCULARS

Just having two eyes doesn't automatically guarantee depth perception—eye placement is key as well. Human eyes face forward, which provides the eyes with the overlap that they need for truly useful stereo vision. Useful for what?

Well, playing sports, for one thing. Stereo vision lets you judge distances between you and other objects—like an oncoming fastball—so you can hit it, catch it, or duck!

IT'S A TRICK

How does any of this relate to 3D movies? Movies usually have a single image projected onto a big screen. The image is flat, so both eyes get the same information. Films that use 3D trick the eye (and the brain) into thinking that objects are

leaping off the screen. The first 3D films were made in the 1950s. They used simple technology. Moviegoers were given glasses with one red lens and one blue (or green) lens. The movie projected onto the screen had two images filmed slightly apart. One image was projected in red and the other in blue (or green). The colored lenses in the glasses filtered out the images projected in their color while letting the other get through. So each eye received a slightly different image, and the brain put them together like it usually does to provide the 3D effect. People loved it—until they realized that most early 3D movies stank.

COMIN' AT YA!

In the early 1980s, 3D films used polarization to work the three-dimensional magic. Filmgoers were given glasses in which each lens had a different polarization—meaning the lens would allow certain types of light in, but not others. Once again, two images were projected onto the screen, each with a different polarity. But once again, 3D was killed, not by the technology, but by stink-o movies like *Jaws 3* (a.k.a. Jaws 3D) and *Comin' At Ya!*

TWO FOR ONE

When you sit down to watch a 3D movie today, you're actually seeing two movies playing at the same time. That's right! Two projectors are running. Light from one projector is polarized

Bwana Devil, the first 3D movie, opened in New York in 1953.

left-right and the other up-down. (That's why the screen looks blurry when you take the glasses off.) The 3D glasses separate the two images, allowing the left-projector movie to go to your left eye and the right-projector movie to your right eye. But two projectors perfectly synced cost a lot of money.

LOOK, MA! NO GLASSES

The latest idea for 3D movies comes out of South Korea. It uses only one projector with a filter over the movie screen. A gadget in front of the projector would polarize the light. Then the filter would block out different regions of the screen, like the slats of window blinds, but vertical instead of horizontal. Each of your eyes would have some of the screen blocked and some of the screen visible. The movie would have the right-eye and left-eye images spliced together in vertical columns. If it works, movie companies may soon be serving up 3D blockbusters with popcorn...but without those annoying glasses!

VIRAL VIDEO: In November 2002, 15-year-old Ghyslain Raza made a video of himself in his school's video lab. He was swinging a golf-ball retriever like a Star Wars lightsaber. Some classmates found the tape and e-mailed it to their friends. Then, one of them posted it on the Internet. The video went viral. Pretty soon Raza couldn't step into the hallway at school without his classmates chanting "Star Wars kid! Star Wars kid!" He was so embarrassed, he dropped out of school. His parents sued three of his classmates for $250,000 in damages, and the term "cyberbullying" was coined with him in mind. In time, Raza overcame his humiliation. And the lawsuit helped him settle on a career: He's studying to become a lawyer. (Watch out cyberbullies!)

"Rock 'n' roll is not so much a question of electric guitars as it is striped pants."

—David Lee Roth (Van Halen frontman)

AUDUBON SHOCKER: John James Audubon was a pioneer of American wildlife conservation. The 19th-century naturalist spent days at a time searching for birds in the woods so he could paint them. In 1905, the National Audubon Society was founded in his honor. Here's what you may not know: Audubon found the birds he wanted to paint, and then...he shot them. His paintings were so realistic because he used "freshly-killed models held in lifelike poses by wires." Sometimes he shot dozens of birds just to paint a single picture.

⤳ FUN FACT ⤶

IN CHINA, THE MOVIE *KINDERGARTEN COP* WAS CALLED *DEVIL KING OF CHILDREN*.

THE HINKUM-BOOBY: In 1857, the religious sect known as the Shakers had a popular song and dance. The lyrics? "I put my right hand in, I put my right hand out; in, out, shake it all about." The song and gestures went on to include the left hand, left and right feet, and the head...just like the modern-day Hokey Pokey.

Bad Movie Science

THE DAY AFTER TOMORROW (2004)

Premise: The Gulf Stream, an Atlantic ocean current that helps regulate Earth's temperature, has become so affected by global climate change that it stops. That causes the ocean to rise and massive icy tidal waves flood New York City. Within days, North America is a frozen wasteland.

Bad Science: Global climate change can affect the Gulf Stream and the oceans, but not that fast. For New York City to flood as it did in the movie, the entire continent of Antarctica would have to melt. For that to happen, all of the sunlight that hits Earth would have to be collectively beamed at the South Pole...for three years.

Premise: After machines take over the world, the human resistance "scorches the sky" to block out the machines' power supply—sunlight. The machines resort to turning humans into "batteries" and using them for power. They're kept alive in a vegetative state while their brains "live" in a virtual reality simulation. Oh, and the machines liquefy the dead as a food source for the living.

Bad Science: Neither the machines nor the humans seem to understand sustainable energy production. Blocking out sunlight wouldn't stop the machines from using solar power. They could build solar panels in space and get all the power they need. And human energy is inefficient. Only about 35% of the energy from the food we eat converts to mechanical energy. And feeding humans to humans? That can lead to a disease called *kuru*, which causes insanity—which would really mess up that VR simulation.

Premise: After Earth's inner core suddenly stops rotating, the planet's magnetic field collapses. This allows the sun's microwaves to penetrate the atmosphere and cause havoc on the surface. Humanity's only hope is a ragtag group of scientists who must travel down to the center of the planet in an experimental vehicle. Their plan: detonate several nuclear bombs in the hopes of "jump-starting Earth's engine."

Bad Science: If Earth's core—which spins at 550 mph—suddenly stopped rotating, all of its rotational energy would be released into the mantle, and then to the surface. That would cause a massive earthquake that would last for years. Not helpful. Also, microwaves couldn't fry the surface: They're too weak, and they're not even affected by magnetic fields. And building a ship that could withstand the immense pressure inside Earth? We don't have enough room to go into just how impossible that is.

WATERWORLD (1995)

Premise: The surface of Earth has been completely covered in water. In one scene, the Mariner (Kevin Costner) swims around an abandoned underwater city that's revealed to be none other than Denver, Colorado, once known as the "Mile-High City."

"Get your facts first, and then you can distort them as much as you please."
— Mark Twain

Bad Science: If the temperature of Earth increased by 8°F, sea levels would rise by three feet due to melting polar ice caps, which would be ecologically catastrophic. But Denver? The city's elevation is 5,280 feet about sea level. Sea levels could never rise to the point where Denver was completely submerged. Even if all the world's ice melted, the ocean would rise by only 250 feet, submerging many coastal cities, but Denver? Not.

CARTOON MANIA

- Walt Disney's first cartoon character wasn't Mickey Mouse. It was Oswald the Lucky Rabbit.

- Comic-book Smurfs that didn't make it into the cartoon series: Alchemist Smurf, Finance Smurf, Mango Smurf, and Pastrycook Smurf.

- In Denmark, the *Peanuts* cartoon is called *Radiserne* (Radishes).

- Experts say: 46% of all violence on TV happens in cartoons.

- First Japanese cartoon to air in the U.S.? *Astro Boy* (1963).

CHAPTER 14

VROOM!

--- **FUN FACT** ---

ADOLF HITLER'S MERCEDES HAD A FALSE FLOOR
TO MAKE HIM LOOK TALLER.

NO PIT STOPS: Inventor Paul H. Wise of Tucson, Arizona, figured when you gotta go, you gotta go. So he designed a way to conceal a toilet under a passenger seat cushion. The setup includes a built-in privacy curtain. It has a foot pedal flush system, a holding tank beneath the car, and an electric water pump.

RIDE LIKE THE WIND

In his *Book of the Golden Hall Master*, Chinese emperor Liang Yuan-ti (AD 552–554) described a wagon with sails that could carry 30 men and travel hundreds of miles in a day. A larger version, said to hold a thousand men, was built for Chinese emperor Yang in AD 610. In those days farmers across China attached sails to their wheelbarrows and plows to ease their labor. Northern Chinese rigged sails to iceboats with small wheels to sail up and down frozen rivers in the wintertime.

OH, SCOOT! Rising gas prices have inspired people to take another look at two-wheeled rides, especially Vespa scooters. The first Vespa scooter was built in 1946 by an Italian company called Piaggio & Co. By 2000 the Vespa had cornered 20% of the U.S. market. Vespa's not the fastest or the quietest scooter made today. But Vespa has always been one thing—cool. It doesn't hurt that stars such as Sting, Antonio Banderas, Milla Jovovich, Matt Damon, and Owen Wilson ride Vespa scooters on location or vacation.

ARMORED LIMO: Security-obsessed celebrities like Kim Kardashian and football star Terrell Owens like being chauffeured in the Armor Horse Vault XXL. It's like a Brinks truck crossed with an 18-wheeler. It has bulletproof windows and 28 people can ride comfortably. The plush interior has seven TVs, emergency escape hatches, and gun ports. You can rent it for $8,000 per day or own it for only $149,900.

Grrrrrr!

TRICK-OUT YOUR RIDE

You may not have a car yet, but when you get one, here are the accessories Uncle John likes best.

- **CAR TEETH** fit over a car's grille to give your ride a cartoon grin. But not all car smiles are alike: You can choose a friendly opened-mouthed smile, an "Alley Gator" pointy-toothed grin, or a "Mako" shark-toothed smile. Auto Xpressions of Lancaster, California, also offers buckteeth, missing teeth, and, of course, vampire fangs.

- **BULLET HOLE STICKERS** come in a set and can be stuck onto car or truck windows and doors. They're sold by a company called Prank Place which also sells such wonders as the Remote

Control Fart Machine, Cockroach Gum, the Fake Parking Ticket, and the $5 Box of Crap.

- **FRENCH FRY HOLDER**, anyone? If you've ever wondered where to put those greasy fries you ordered at the drive-thru, here's the answer. The Improvements company offers a French Fry Holder with a non-slip rubber base that fits right inside a cup holder. It even has a clip-on ketchup cup for easy dipping.

- **CARLASHES** are giant plastic eyelashes that frame your VW Beetle's headlights. (They also look cute on BMWs and Mini Coopers.)

- **CARSTACHE** is a mustache for your car's grille. It's made of fuzzy fake fur and comes in many colors and styles to match every personality.

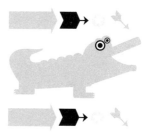

~~~→ **TIRE TRIVIA**

What do you call a strip of tire that's come off and is left on the highway? A "road alligator."

E.T. IS WATCHING! Crackpots aren't the only ones who see UFOs when they scan the sky. Test pilots, astronauts, and even high-ranking military officers have gone on record to report unidentified flying objects. Air Chief Marshal Lord Dowding was a commanding officer in Britain's Royal Air Force during World War II. Here's what he had to say: "More than 10,000 sightings have been reported, the majority of which cannot be accounted for by any 'scientific' explanation... They have been tracked on radar screens and the observed speeds have been as great as 9,000 mph. I am convinced that these objects do exist and they are not manufactured by any nation on earth. I can therefore see no alternative to accepting the theory that they come from an extraterrestrial source."

"I don't laugh at people anymore when they say they've seen UFOs. I've seen one myself."

—President Jimmy Carter, 1976

～～ TRANSFORMERS TRAGEDY

In 2010, wannabe actress Gabriela Cedillo took the day off from her day job at a Chicago bank. The movie *Transformers 3* was filming nearby. And Cedillo wanted to be in it. She was paid $25 to sit in her car while a truck towed another car at high speed in the opposite direction. As the towed car passed, the cable snapped. It whipped through Cedillo's windshield and sliced open her skull. She was airlifted to Loyola University Hospital and underwent brain surgery. The movie company promised to pay Cedillo's medical bills. But her family still sued the film company. Why? The stunt-gone-wrong left Cedillo partially paralyzed and blind in one eye.

LINCOLN'S DEATH TRAIN

This ghostly train puts the "boo" in caboose.

U.S. President Abraham Lincoln was assassinated in April 1865. After his death, a funeral train delivered his body from Washington, D.C., to its final resting place in Springfield, Illinois. Frequent stops were made along the way so that mourners could pay their respects. Each time the train stopped, clocks were stopped in honor of the fallen leader.

Several years later, a rail worker on the line between New York City and Albany (part of the death train's route) was clearing brush late one April night. A chilly wind, "like just before a thunderstorm," swept over the tracks. A "huge blanket of utter darkness" rolled over the man, snuffing out his lantern. Then...a blue glow covered the tracks, followed by the bright headlight of a train.

The man cowered against a tree as a steam engine draped in black crepe emerged out of the darkness. A skeletal orchestra played a dirge from a flat car behind the crewless engine. An identical train followed the first, except this time, in place of the phantom musicians, there was a single black crepe-covered coffin.

Ghostly soldiers wearing blue Union uniforms stood at attention along the track and saluted the casket as it passed. The worker fled back to the Hudson Division station to find that the clocks were all running six minutes late.

Ghostly soldiers stood at attention along the track and saluted the casket as it passed.

Ever since, April always brings reports of people hearing unexplained steam whistles. They see mysterious plumes of smoke and feel chilly winds along the route of the train. To this day, some claim that watches and clocks still stop wherever the ghost train goes.

Flight Trick

WHAT A DRAG

Everything that flies—an airplane, a bird, a butterfly—is subject to the same four forces. To stay up, there must be enough *lift* and *thrust* to overcome *weight* and *drag*. *Thrust* is the power supplied by an engine (for a plane) or by flapping

(for a bird). *Weight* is how gravity affects what's flying. *Drag* is how much whatever is trying to fly is slowed down by friction from the air. But *lift* is the force that keeps the plane or bird from falling out of the sky. How does lift work?

LIFT ME UP

Picture a wing slicing through the air like a knife. Some air goes over it and some under it. Air particles moving *over* the wing take the same amount of time to pass over it as the particles below it take to pass *under* it. So a wing that is curved on top will force the air going over it to travel faster than the air below. The higher air speed makes the air pressure above the wing less than the air pressure below it. The resulting higher pressure below pushes toward the lower pressure above in an attempt to equalize. And the force from below literally "lifts" the wing. With enough lift, anything can be made to fly, no matter how much it weighs.

THE PAPER TRICK

Try this: Drape a square of toilet paper over your fingers. Hold it to your chin just beneath your lower lip. Now blow horizontally over the top of it. See how the paper rises up? That's lift in action. By speeding up the air on top of the toilet paper, you decreased the pressure over it. The higher pressure from below pushed the paper upward toward the area of lower pressure. Result: flight. And the rest is aviation history.

- The world's first drive-through filling station opened for business on June 1, 1912. Where? Columbus, Ohio.

- A gas station is a *petrol bunk* in India, a *petrol kiosk* in Singapore, and a *servo* in Australia.

- Germany, France, and England all pay a 70% gas tax. Americans pay only a 23% gas tax.

- If aircraft carriers ran on gasoline, they'd get about 6 inches to the gallon.

- *Eww!* Used diapers and turkey guts are now being considered as alternative fuel sources.

CHAPTER 15

WEATHER OR NOT...

THE MASSACHUSETTS INSTITUTE OF TECHNOLOGY USES
STORMWATER RUNOFF TO FLUSH ITS TOILETS.

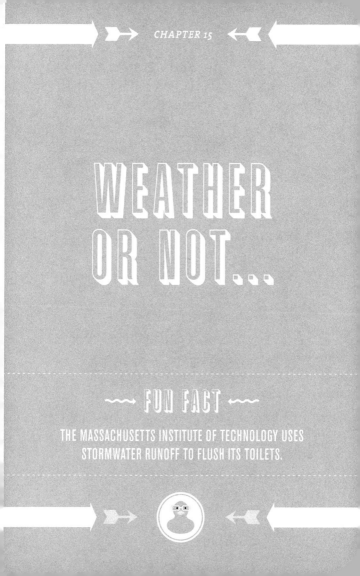

Americans often check travel alerts before visiting other countries. Good idea. But what about the good old U.S.A.? The Australian government's travel advisory website says, "Many parts of the United States are subject to earthquakes, wildfires, floods, extreme heat, hurricanes, mudslides, landslides, thunderstorms and lightning, tornadoes, tsunamis, volcanoes, freezing rain, heavy snow and blizzards, and extreme cold." (Yikes!)

~~~ GROANER ~~~

DID YOU HEAR ABOUT THE HURRICANE THAT LOST ITS FORCE? IT WAS DISGUSTED.

BLUE SKIES: Want to know if the weather will be clear? Watch for high-flying sparrows. Insects fly higher when the air pressure is high (high pressure means fine weather). And swallows fly higher to catch and eat them.

EARTHQUAKE WEATHER: Rumor says that big earthquakes always hit in the morning when it's hot and dry. True? No. The belief that earthquakes hit when the weather is hot and dry began with the ancient Greek philosopher, Aristotle (384–322 BCE). Aristotle theorized that earthquakes were caused by air trapped underground. Before one hit, he thought, so much air would be trapped that the air above ground would be hot and calm. We now know that earthquakes are caused by tectonic plates shifting below the earth's surface. Neither the weather nor the time of day has any affect on them. Big earthquakes have been recorded at all times of the day and night, year round.

∿ RED SKY AT MORNING

You may have heard someone say, "Red sky at morning, sailor take warning." Guess what? The old saying is true! A red sunrise is caused by light shining on moist clouds, a sign of wind and rain coming in from the west.

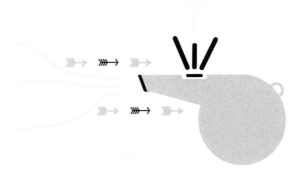

- A whistle sounds louder just before it rains.

- Average life span of an umbrella: 1 1/2 years.

- You can use pinecones to forecast rain. When rain is on the way, the scales close.

- A drizzle is 14 drops of rain per square foot per second; a light rain is 26 drops.

- According to weather forecasters, "scattered showers" means a 10 percent chance of rain.

- Cherrapunji, India, is the wettest inhabited place on earth, with 428 inches of rain per year.

- The *Simpsons* cartoonist Matt Groening's name rhymes with "raining."

A lot of people seem to talk about the weather when they have nothing else to say. If you want a different kind of chitchat, head for the Moon. The Moon has no wind, no sunshine, no clouds, no rain, no hurricanes, no twisters...no weather at all. If you happen to be on the Moon and need a conversation starter, try asking this question:

How long do you think it would take to pedal your bike to the Moon? (Answer: 3 years)

~~~ FUN FACT ~~~

WEARING A HAT WILL KEEP YOUR FEET WARM
IN COLD WEATHER.

Legend says that a Chinese woman invented the umbrella 3,000 years ago. The basic design has never changed. But that hasn't stopped inventors and mad scientists from trying to "improve" on it. The United States Patent and Trademark Office has received thousands of applications for umbrella patents. Examples include a weather-forecasting umbrella, a glow-in-the-dark umbrella, a strap-on umbrella for pets, a *Star Wars* style lightsaber umbrella, and an electric stun-gun umbrella. The patent office has four full-time employees who do nothing but process umbrella claims.

LIGHTNING TRIVIA

- A bolt of lightning is six times hotter than the sun.

- Lightning can heat the air around it to temperatures of more than 50,000°F.

- Odds of being killed by lightning are about the same as being killed falling out of bed.

THE "DON'T FLUSH ME" PROJECT

During heavy storms, rainwater rushes through New York City's sewers. Millions of gallons of untreated sewage floods from the sewers into New York Harbor. A college student named Leif Percifield came up with a solution: During rainstorms, don't flush! A sensor connected to a cell phone tracks water levels in the city's sewer system. When the levels rise close to the point of overflowing, the cell phone calls a computer. The computer sends out text messages and Twitter tweets telling New Yorkers not to flush until the crisis passes.

WATERMELON SNOW:
If you're ever high up in a snowy mountain range and come across bright, pink snow, don't worry. You're not seeing things. It's caused by tiny organisms called *Chlamydomonas nivalis*. They're a species of algae that loves the cold (*nivalis* means "snowy" in Latin). The algae protects itself from harsh light coming off the snow by oozing out a slimy gel. The gel turns pink in sunlight. Caution: Never eat watermelon snow. (Duh!) It causes diarrhea.

- Even if the sky overhead is clear, lightning from a storm as many as 25 miles away can still strike you. And thunder always comes with lightning. It just might be too far away for you to hear.

- During a "superstorm" in March 1993, more than 44 million acre-feet of snow and rain fell on the East Coast of the United States. That's an area of volume equal to one acre, one foot deep.

- 90 percent of avalanches happen within 24 hours of a snowstorm. An avalanche can send millions of tons of snow down a hill at speeds of 200 miles per hour.

- One of the worst droughts ever recorded occurred in Sichuan Province in China in 1936. Five million people died and more than 30 million farms were destroyed.

- It's rare, but large fires can cause thunderstorms. How? If the heat from the fire collides with cool temperatures in the upper atmosphere, *boom!*

- A "heat burst" happens when a downdraft of warm air replaces the cool air beneath it. That instantly raises the temperature, but not for long. A heat burst in Kimberly, South Africa, boosted the temperature 43°F in just five minutes. Forty minutes later, the temperature had dropped back to normal.

- Temperatures in Oymyakon, Siberia, sometimes dip to an low of -96°F. That makes it the coldest place on Earth. At that temperature, a person's breath freezes in mid-air and hangs there.

- Hurricanes, cyclones, and other large weather systems in the Northern Hemisphere always rotate in a counterclockwise direction. Those in the Southern Hemisphere rotate clockwise. What happens to a hurricane when it moves from one hemisphere to another? Nothing. Hurricanes never leave their hemispheres of origin.

Tornado!

In 1971, University of Chicago professor
Dr. Tetsuya Fujita created a scale to classify
the destructive power of tornadoes. He broke
the scale into six categories based on wind speed.
Here's the "Fujita Tornado Scale" breakdown:

- F0, 40–72 mph: breaks branches off trees.

- F1, 73–112 mph: overturns mobile homes.

- F2, 113–157 mph: tears roofs off houses.

- F3, 158–206 mph: turns over trains.

- F4, 207–260 mph: levels houses.

- F5, 261–318 mph: turns cars into missiles.

The most powerful tornado
on record, so far,
was an F5. It swept
through Oklahoma
on May 3, 1999, and
had a top wind
speed of 302 mph.

Actress Judy Garland
played Dorothy in
The Wizard of Oz.
On the day she died,
a tornado touched
down in Kansas.

CHAPTER 16

UNDERWEAR!

~~ FUN FACT ~~

KING TUT WAS BURIED WITH 145 PAIRS
OF LOINCLOTH UNDERWEAR.

UNDIES ON THE HEAD: Maternity wards in Sweden are using underpants as caps for newborn babies. Why? Because when they use real baby caps, people steal them. "We got tired of buying new caps all the time," said one nurse. So they started using adult hospital-issue underwear instead. She said if you roll up the underpants nicely on the baby's tiny head, it doesn't look that bad.

UNDERWEAR AFFAIR: The Underwear Affair is a charity race held in Canada to raise awareness for cancers that occur below the waist—including prostate, ovarian, testicular, bladder, and colorectal cancers. Weeks ahead of the race, volunteers promote the event by wearing skivvies (underwear) over their clothing. On race day, participants run the 10k race or walk the 5k walk in their underwear or in underwear-themed costumes. It's all about "Bringing a little awareness to down there-ness."

DISNEY DRAWERS: Those costumed characters you see walking around at Disney World aren't always as happy as they look. Some costumes hug the body so tightly it makes regular underwear bunch up. (Can you say wedgie?) To prevent unsightly VLPs (visible panty lines), the company supplies underwear for costumed employees to wear: athletic supporters, tights or cycling shorts. Problem? Employees are not issued their own undergarments. Everyone has to *share*. Disney is supposed to launder the undies in hot water before passing them on to the next wearer. But that wasn't happening. Workers finally had enough. "I don't want to share my underwear," said stilt walker Gary Stevenson. The workers sued Disney World for the right to wear their own undies while on duty. They won.

~~~➳ **SEEN ON A BUMPER STICKER**

Follow your dreams, except that one where you're at school in your underwear.

Canada's Captain Underpants

Brent King is a mechanical engineer in Calgary, the largest city in the province of Alberta. Like many big cities, Calgary has a homelessness problem. King wanted to help. So he visited an organization called the Mustard Seed. King asked if there was anything special they needed. There was: men's underwear.

Seems it's common for people to give used clothing to homeless shelters and thrift shops. But used underwear? That's not the kind of thing that gets donated. And not many people think of donating *new* underwear, so homeless shelters rarely have enough.

King formed a charity called Got Ginch ("ginch" is a slang term for men's briefs). He funded it with thousands of dollars of his own money, plus thousands more raised from friends. Rather than buy underwear at retail prices, he asked a business associate in China to help him work directly with a textile mill overseas to save money.

THE GREAT GINCH DRIVE

Next, King decided to fill an RV full of underwear. He spent his summer vacation driving 3,600 miles across Canada from Vancouver to Halifax, Nova Scotia. He handed out underwear to homeless shelters in 10 different cities as he went. By the time he finished his Cross-Canada Underwear Drive a few weeks later, he'd given away more than 25,000 pairs of men's briefs.

He did it again the following summer, this time raising enough money to give away 30,000 pairs of underwear. The cross-country tours have helped raise awareness of the underwear issue, and many Canadian homeless shelters have reported increased underwear donations.

In case you think women don't need undies, too, there's now a second charity: Need Knickers. Its goal: to deliver new underwear (knickers) for women to homeless shelters across Canada.

UNDERWEAR IN SPACE: In 2009, Koichi Wakata became the first Japanese astronaut to live on the International Space Station. Although few people knew it, he was making history of another kind as well: He went an entire month without changing his underwear. That's the longest voluntary stretch of underpants-wearing in the history of human spaceflight. Luckily for everyone else on the space station, these were no ordinary underpants. They were water-absorbing, antibacterial, odor-eliminating, quick-drying, flame-resistant, anti-static experimental "J-Wear." The Japanese space agency designed the undies to be worn by astronauts for weeks on end without causing discomfort to the wearer (or to others in the vicinity). "I wore them for about a month, and my crew members never complained," said Wakata. "So I think the experiment went fine."

~~~ FUN FACT ~~~

NAVY SEALS IN VIETNAM SOMETIMES WORE PANTYHOSE...
TO KEEP LEECHES OFF.

~~~> **UNDER-EASE:** An inventor named Buck Weimer came up with very special underpants. They contain a powerful charcoal filter that removes the stinky smell of intestinal gas. (Yes, we're talking about farts.) They're made from an airtight fabric and have an "exit hole" for farts. The hole is fitted with a removable charcoal filter. Each pair lasts for up to six months. But the filter has to be changed every month or two, "depending on the amount and strength of the gas being released." Under-Ease cost $24.95 a pair, but if you buy a pair don't think you can fart in secret. They don't take care of the *sound* of farts. Just the smell.

WANDERING COMRADE: In 1995, the Russian presidential delegation made a state visit to Washington, D.C. In the middle of the night, Secret Service agents found a man standing in the middle of Pennsylvania Avenue in his underwear. It was Russian President Boris Yeltsin. He was trying to hail a cab and go get pizza.

Uncovering Underwear History

Ever wondered what people once wore beneath their togas and hoopskirts? Here's a peek.

WHEN IN ANCIENT ROME...OR EGYPT

- Roman noblemen wore tunics and briefs under their togas. Women wore tunics, too. But they also wore breastbands to make them fashionably flat-chested.

- Egyptian men wore loincloths beneath their robes. What's a loincloth? Imagine a large cloth diaper...for adults.

TOO BREEZY FOR THE LADIES

- In the 1800s fashionable ladies wanted to have tiny little waists. To get an hourglass shape, they wore corsets that were stiffened with iron rods or whalebone. Corsets were laced so tight that some women's ribs actually broke.

- Most women didn't wear panties of any kind until the mid-1830s. Before that, pants were considered too masculine.

- The hoopskirts of the 1850s and 1860s created a problem. The stiff frame that gave the skirt its shape flew up in a high wind. Women started wearing baggy cotton "drawers." They came down below the knee and were tied at the waist with a drawstring. Some were so enormous they looked like they were made for a giantess.

BOXERS, BRIEFS, OR SKIRTS?

- In Scotland, men have been wearing pleated, knee-length wool skirts called *kilts* since the 1500s. Britain's Prince Charles often wears one. Bagpipers always wear them. So what does a Scotsman wear under his kilt? Absolutely nothing.

- Men didn't wear boxers or briefs before the 20th century. They wore longjohns. These one-piece garments buttoned up the front and had a little drop door that unbuttoned in the back.

- In earlier days, the long tails of men's shirts did double duty as underpants.

THE ROYAL KNICKERS

England's Queen Elizabeth II isn't the kind of person who has to pack her own suitcases or do her laundry when traveling abroad. But there may be times when she wishes she was. In 2012, a pair of silk undies went up for auction on eBay. They were left aboard a plane used by the Queen during a 1968 visit to Chile. The underwear, monogrammed with an "E" for Elizabeth and a crown, had somehow fallen into the hands of a Hungarian Baron. The Baron kept them for more than 40 years. When he died in the summer of 2010, his heirs made plans to put the royal undies up for auction. The opening bid for the queen's knickers: $4,000. And the royal undies sold for... a whopping $18,101.

CHAPTER 17

SPACE CADETS

IN SPACE, FISH SWIM IN LOOPS RATHER
THAN STRAIGHT LINES.

CAN YOU HEAR ME NOW? No matter what you may have seen in science-fiction films, there is no sound in space. Period. Sound needs some kind of material—air, water, bedroom walls—to travel through. Slam your hand down on your desk and the molecules that make up the desk will vibrate. The vibrating desk molecules will make the air molecules around them vibrate which will cause the air molecules next to *them* to vibrate...and a sound wave will travel through the air. Slam your hand on the outside of a spaceship door while it's in space, and the molecules in the door will vibrate—but there are no air molecules in space, so no sound waves can form. (The people inside could hear the noise, though, because there *is* air inside the craft.)

~~~ FUN FACT ~~~

ACCORDING TO ASTRONAUTS' NOTES, MOON DUST SMELLS LIKE EXPLODED FIRECRACKERS.

ROCKET-RAM: In the early 1800s, rockets were all the rage—mostly in the form of unguided but terrifying weapons raining down from above. However, inventor Claude Ruggieri had a better idea: a rocket for launching people into the air. His individual rockets were too small to support the weight of a human. So Ruggieri devised a "rocket necklace"—clusters of rockets festooning a metal chamber that all went off at the same time. In 1830, Ruggieri launched a ram (as in male sheep) 600 feet into the air and landed it safely with a parachute. When Paris police caught wind of Ruggieri's next plan—to send up a small child—they put a stop to his experiments.

～～SNORE NO MORE

Astronauts who snore on Earth do not snore in space.

～～PEE-UUW

International Space Station astronauts change their underwear only twice a week.

E.T. PLAYLIST

In 1977, NASA launched two unmanned *Voyager* spacecrafts to explore the outer reaches of the galaxy. Both ships carried an interstellar audio greeting from earthlings to any alien life-form that might be encountered. On board each craft was a gold-plated phonograph record containing songs selected by a NASA committee chaired by cosmologist and best-selling author Carl Sagan. Songs were chosen to represent Earth's best musical mix. If the aliens can get their hands (tentacles?) on an old-fashioned turnable, these are some of the songs they'll hear:

- "Johnny B. Goode," performed by Chuck Berry

- Zaire pygmy girls' initiation song

- Australian aborigine songs "Morning Star" and "Devil Bird"

- Mexican song "El Cascabel," performed by Lorenzo Barcelata and the Mariachi México

- Azerbaijani bagpipes, recorded by Radio Moscow

- "Melancholy Blues," performed by Louis Armstrong and his Hot Seven

- Peruvian panpipes and drum

- Mozart's "Queen of the Night" aria from *The Magic Flute*

- New Guinean men's house song

- Japanese song "Tsuru No Sugomori" ("Crane's Nest")

- Navajo Indian, "Night Chant," recorded by Willard Rhodes

- "Dark Was the Night," written and performed by Blind Willie Johnson

Earthlings interested in the Voyager Gold Record can hear most of the songs online.

SPACE PANELS: In space, the sun never stops shining and it's not filtered through Earth's thick atmosphere. Seems like the perfect place to produce power using solar panels. Why hasn't anyone done it yet? No one has figured out a cost-effective way to get the energy down to the planet's surface. One idea is to "beam" it down using microwaves. If that idea works, space panels could become a new power source.

DISARMING NEWTS: In 1985, Soviet scientists decided to send 10 Iberian ribbed newts into space. First, they cut off the newts front limbs (Ouch!). The purpose of this animal amputation? They wanted to study whether the missing limbs would regenerate in zero gravity the same way they do on Earth. The newts were launched into space aboard the biomedical research mission satellite *Bion 7*. By watching the limbs grow back (or not) the scientists hoped to learn how humans might recover from injuries in space.

LITTLE COTTAGE ON THE MOON

Small red cottages are a common sight in Sweden. Now the country wants to put one on the Moon. In 2006, Sweden held a nationwide contest for children to design the cottage. It had to be very small—no more than eight square meters and weighing no more than 10 pounds. The winning cottage is really a machine designed for landing on the moon. The lander will fly to the Moon "as usual." Once it has landed, it will cover itself with an inflatable shell which will make it look like a little red cottage. "We know where the Americans want to land people in 2020," said project designer Mikael Genberg. "It would be nice if we had a house for them when they come."

"The dinosaurs became extinct because they didn't have a space program. And if we become extinct because we don't have a space program, it'll serve us right!"

—Larry Niven

Home, Home on...the Moon

In 2007, a team of 30 astronomers, engineers, and students from around the world unveiled a plan for a project called Luna Gaia (Moon Earth). The plan calls for a Moon complex that would be 95% self-sufficient. Those living there would need little help from Earth to survive.

• The complex would consist of inflatable "pods" the size of small apartments. They would be made of a durable Kevlar-like material and linked by inflatable tunnels. The first installation would be built in a mile-wide crater near the Moon's north pole. This would protect inhabitants from solar radiation.

• A dozen 100-foot-wide mirrors on the crater's rim would direct sunlight to a power station. That light would heat water to produce steam. Steam would drive turbines, as in a typical power plant.

• Some of the pods would be greenhouses for

growing food. Plants would provide oxygen for breathing. Other pods would house aquariums where fast-growing fish could provide food.

• Bath water would be filtered and treated to convert it back to drinking water. And so would urine (pee).

• There would be zero waste. All refuse, including human waste, would be broken down by microbes and turned into fertilizer for plants.

• NASA has already announced plans to build a lunar post around 2020.

Flintstones vs. Jetsons

Would Stone Age Man or Space Age Man have the biggest carbon footprint? We think the middle-class lives of two famous cartoon characters, Fred Flintstone and George Jetson, offer a few insights.

FRED FLINTSTONE

• The Flintstone family lives in the Stone Age. All building materials, tools, cars, and consumer goods are made from a very eco-friendly material—stone. Fred Flintstone lives off the Earth, literally.

• Flintstone doesn't use fossil fuels. He lives alongside plants and animals that will one day putrefy and *become* petroleum. Without a drop of oil, Flintstone powers his car by rapidly pedaling his feet, perhaps the greenest alternative energy source in history.

• Fred doesn't wear shoes or socks or even pants. That ugly orange polka-dotted "dress" he wears appears to have been made from animal skins. That means he doesn't contribute to the pesticide-dependent cotton industry. Conclusion: Fred's clothes are quite "green."

• Since electricity hasn't been harnessed yet, all the appliances in his home are powered by birds and other animals. (Like the Bird Record Player—the tip of the bird's pointy beak plays the record as it spins on the back of a turtle.) Looks like the Flintstone family's carbon footprint is *zero*.

Fred Flintstone: "I wouldn't know what to wear to a monster bash." Barney Rubble: "In your case, Fred, a monster bash is a come-as-you-are party."

GEORGE JETSON

• The Jetson family lives in a future filled with technology and labor-saving devices, from flying cars to self-cleaning kitchens, and robot dogs.

• Jetson eats food prepared by a Food-a-Rac-a-Cycle. It's a microwave-size machine that makes meals at the push of a button. What kind of food is in a Jetson meal: "Blobs of tasteless but nutritious paste" with chemicals added for flavor. None of it is locally grown or organic.

• The Jetson family (George, his boy Elroy, daughter Judy, and Jane his wife) enjoys many gadgets and gizmos. They have talking watches, machines to control their dreams, holographic 3D

television, video phones, a machine that gets them out of bed and dresses them, and Rosie, a robot maid. Every one of these gadgets requires electricity— a lot of it!

• Jetson drives a flying car that looks like a cross between a Volkswagen Beetle and a flying saucer. The closest vehicle we have today is a Sikorsky S-76C, a commercial helicopter that gets two miles per gallon. The gas-guzzling Hummer HS gets about 10 mpg, so Jetson's "futuristic" car is only 20% as efficient as a Hummer.

• Jetson needs that flying car because he lives in a sky-high apartment. All of the buildings in his hometown of Orbit City are hundreds of feet above the ground. Why? No one knows for sure. Maybe by 2062—the year the cartoon takes place—all the electricity used to power *our* labor-saving devices will have spewed so much carbon into the air that the polar ice caps melted, covering Earth's surface with water, and forcing humanity to build upward. (Sorry, George! Our bad.) As for the Jetson family's carbon footprint: *astronomically* big.

"The future is made of the same stuff as the present."
—Simone Weil

~~~ FUN FACT ~~~

ASTRONAUT BUZZ ALDRIN CLAIMS TO HAVE BEEN THE FIRST MAN TO PEE IN HIS PANTS ON THE MOON.

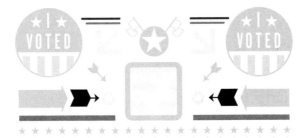

ONLY THE SMALL SURVIVE

The space shuttle *Columbia* disintegrated over Texas during its reentry on February 1, 2003. Its seven crew members weren't the only ones to meet a tragic end. The shuttle also carried silkworms, golden orb spiders, carpenter bees, Japanese killifish, and harvester ants in a gel-filled ant farm. The only known survivors? Microscopic nematodes (roundworms) that were found intact in the debris.

- Astronauts get "spacesick" so often that the space shuttle toilet has a special setting for vomit.

- In 1997, astronaut John Blaha became the first American to vote from space.

CHAPTER 18

BATHROOM MANIA

~~~ FUN FACT ~~~

NOVEMBER 19 IS WORLD TOILET DAY.

DON'T BREATHE IN THE BATHROOM

In February 2011, the Federal Aviation Agency ordered every U.S. airline to dismantle the oxygen generators (those things that drop out of the ceiling if the plane loses cabin pressure) in airplane bathrooms. Apparently, the government is worried that terrorists might be able to use the equipment to start a fire or set off a bomb in the bathroom. So are you doomed if the plane loses pressure while you're on the pot? No, but you may be embarrassed: As soon as the flight attendants put on their own oxygen masks, they will unlock the bathrooms and pass bottles of oxygen in to those caught with their pants down.

~~~ FUN FACT ~~~

WALT DISNEY WORLD GOES THROUGH ABOUT
194,871 MILES OF TOILET PAPER EACH YEAR.

PEE AND PLAY: Sega is trying out a new video game system: the Sega Toylet. In early 2011, Sega installed Toylet game consoles in a few public restrooms in Tokyo, Japan. Here's how the game works: A pressure sensor is installed inside a urinal. A video display is installed at eye level above it. "Players" aim for the sensor as they make use of the facilities. So far, Toylets are experimental. And Sega says it has "no plans to turn them into actual products."

REUSABLE TOILET WIPES?

A company called Wallypop sells reusable toilet wipes. They're made from flannel and terrycloth, and they're for people who feel guilty about using toilet paper. Wallypop's tips for cleaning the wipes? Just "shake, scrape, swish, or squirt off anything you don't want in your laundry." But—the company warns—"be sure to wash the cloths separately from other laundry." The company promises, "This is not nearly as gross as you might be imagining." (Yes…yes, it is!)

It's the first toilet, says the manufacturer, made for "modern Americans." (Huh?) Translation: It's extra-large. Invented by the Great John Toilet Company (no relation to Uncle John), the Great John has a wider base than other toilets to provide extra support. The base connects to the bathroom floor with four anchors instead of the usual two. The seat provides 150 percent more "contact area" than a normal toilet. It also offers "side wings" to prevent pinching if flesh still hangs over the seat. How much weight can the Great John take? It can support a person up to the weight of 2,000 pounds.

SPARKLE BRITE!

Jemal Wright Bath Designs makes fancy toilets and matching bathroom fixtures. So far, Wright has made diamond-encrusted toilets, a gold-plated toilet with a matching pedestal sink, and a metallic orange chrome toilet...with a diamond-encrusted flush handle. Cost: $65,000...and up.

LAND OF ENCHANTED TOILETS

New Mexico's nickname is the "Land of Enchantment." The name refers to the state's scenic beauty, which includes Toilet Rock, a natural rock formation shaped like a flush toilet.

Toilet Terror

Did your parents ever tell you about the monster that lives in the closet? In Japan parents warn children that a hairy hand will rise up out of the toilet bowl and drag them down into the abyss it if they're naughty.

In 2009, a bestselling Japanese horror writer named Koji Suzuki decided to use that superstition. He wrote a terrifying tale about a goblin who lives in a public restroom. Then, he made a deal with a paper company to "publish" his story...on rolls of toilet paper.

The story—titled "Drop"—is printed on toilet paper in blue ink with red, blood-like splatters. It takes up only three feet of toilet paper and is meant to be read in a single sitting. Priced at 210 yen (about $2.00), each roll contains several copies of the story so that more than one person gets to read it. The rolls are marketed as "Japan's scariest toilet paper."

BEWARE OF THE HAIRY HAND!

ALLIGATOR: After a night away, Alexis Dunbar returned to her Palmetto, Florida, home and went to the bathroom. She was greeted by a hiss from a seven-foot-long alligator. She screamed, closed the door, and called wildlife officials, who came and took it away. Dunbar told reporters the alligator came in through her cat door. Her two cats were fine, but the gator had rearranged all the furniture.

DEER: Colleen Slattery and Beau Williams were sitting in their apartment in Eagan, Minnesota, one morning when they were startled by a huge crash. A deer had smashed through their bathroom window. The couple found the deer with both of its front legs stuck in the toilet bowl. Police officers got the deer out of the toilet, guided it outside, and watched as it ran away.

SPIDER: One night, Christopher Robinson of Clacton-on-Sea, England, was called to the bathroom by his wife, Janine. She told Christopher there was a spider in the bathroom. Wanting to play the good husband, he chased the spider around the bathroom, cornered it behind the toilet and—having no bug spray handy—sprayed deodorant. Not sure he'd killed the spider, he leaned closer and lit his lighter so he could see. The helpful husband must have forgotten that fire and aerosol spray makes an explosive mix. He was blown out of the bathroom and into the hallway. The explosion scorched the bathroom and left Christopher with burns on his legs and arms. A fireman said there was no sign of the spider.

POWER TO THE POOPLE: Experts say that before long, we may be filling our cars with fuel made from chicken poop, pig poop, or even human poop. Poo-fuel will cost about 10 cents a gallon and offer better mileage. Some large poultry and pig farms have already begun to use poop for power. A plant in western Minnesota converts 700,000 tons of turkey droppings per year into electricity. A plant in the Netherlands plans to power 90,000 homes using chicken waste. And human waste treatment plants could soon become sources of perpetual poo power.

Rescuing Poo Girl

When it's your turn to be famous for 15 minutes, let's hope toilets are not involved.

TO THE LOO...AND BEYOND

In August 2009, a 19-year-old British girl named Charlotte Taylor hopped a train to the city of Leeds, England. She and some friends had tickets to a three-day music festival featuring bands such as Radiohead, Vampire Weekend, the Yeah Yeah Yeahs, Kings of Leon, and the Arctic Monkeys.

Taylor made it to the festival and was enjoying the music along with thousands of other fans. Then nature called, but when she visited the portable toilets, she accidentally dropped her purse down the toilet.

OH, NOOO!

Taylor had a wad of cash in her purse (about $650). Her new iPhone was in there. So were her house keys and the train ticket she needed to get home. As she watched her purse fall into the toilet, Taylor felt she had only one option: get it back.

First she reached into the hole with one arm, feeling for her purse. No luck. Then she tried two arms. Still no luck. So she stuck her head and shoulders down through the toilet bowl, too. That's when she got stuck.

IN THE STINK OF IT

Taylor struggled to free herself. All she managed to do was wedge herself deeper into the bowl. Her friends waiting outside couldn't get inside to free her. Finally the fire department had to be called.

Once the firefighters arrived word spread throughout the music festival. A crowd formed around the porta-john, chanting, "POO GIRL! POO GIRL!"

It took seven firefighters to dismantle the portable toilet and set Taylor free. In all, she spent nearly 30 minutes wedged upside down in the john. The helpful firefighters hosed her down, and—after changing into dry clothes—Taylor went back to enjoying the music.

Celebrities in... the Can

Leonardo DiCaprio. While attending a soccer game at the World Cup in South Africa in the  summer of 2010, DiCaprio left the stands to use the bathroom. To his horror, a bunch of fans spotted him and followed him in. DiCaprio tried to find some privacy by running into a stall, but there were too many men—and women—in the bathroom, crowding around to peek into it. They started shaking the stall walls and nearly toppled them onto DiCaprio, which would have put him at the bottom of a pile of gaping fans. But DiCaprio screamed for help and security officers came to his rescue.

Miley Cyrus. When Barbara Walters interviews celebrities for her Oscar-night specials, she films in the celebrity's home to create warmth. When she and her crew came to Cyrus's home in 2008, they made themselves a little too much at home. They used her bathrooms...and clogged up all the toilets. Cyrus had no hard feelings—she called a plumber and later even sent Walters a tiny solid-gold toilet.

Jackie Chan. He's a fervent environmentalist, and he takes that attitude with him to movie sets. Addressing a crowd at a "Green Living" rally in Singapore in 2009, Chan insisted that members of the film crew save water by going to the bathroom in groups. Only after the last one finishes up, he explained, can the toilet be flushed. Chan calls it the "Golden Flush."

- Americans use enough toilet paper each year to stretch to the Sun and back.

- Hawaiians once used coconut husks for toilet paper.

- Shaquille O'Neal's 20,000-square-foot mansion has remote-control toilets.

- Only 7% of homes in Afghanistan have a flush toilet, but 19% have a television.

- Bathroom readers beware: Fine for leaving a public toilet unflushed in Singapore—$150.

CHAPTER 19

BODY PARTS

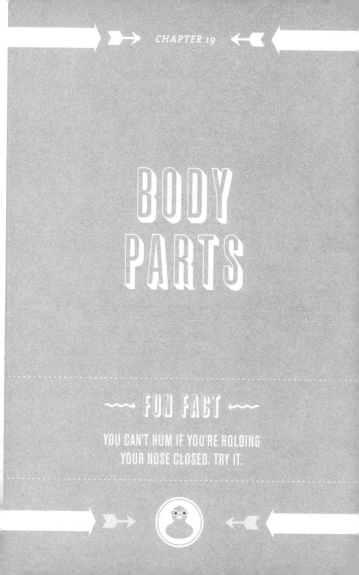

TAKE A NAP! Naps aren't just for toddlers anymore. Scientists have found two big peaks in our need for sleep—at 3 a.m. and 3 p.m. The first is dead in the center of our sleep cycle. But the second is smack in the middle of the day. What does this mean? We should all be napping in midafternoon. At present, only 38% of us do.

SLEEP TIGHT TIPS!

- Exercise before going to bed.

- Go to bed about the same time each night.

- Avoid drinking anything except warm milk.

- No illuminated clocks. (They just remind you that you can't get to sleep.)

- Keep your bedroom dark and slightly cool (about 65°F is best).

LONGEST NAME FOR A MUSCLE

Levator Labii Superioris Alaeque Nasi. It's a two-inch muscle between your nose and upper lip.

AN ARM AND A LEG: In 2003, the *South China Morning Post* reported that a 19-year-old security guard from Changsha, Hunan province, was selling himself—one piece at a time. The young man put posters up advertising his body parts for sale to the highest bidder: $18,000 for a kidney and $9,000 for an eye. Why would anyone sell their own body parts? He wanted to "get rich."

China banned the trading of human organs in 2007, but that hasn't put a stop to it. In 2012, a 17-year-old student from Huaishan City, in the Chinese province of Anhui, decided to sell his own kidney for 22,000 yuan (about $3,400). Why? So he could buy an iPhone and an iPad 2. Only a fraction of the people who need organ transplants in China are able to get them, leading to a thriving black market for human organs.

"What a waste it is to lose one's mind. Or to not have a mind is being very wasteful. How true it is."

—Dan Quayle, U.S. Vice President

- All the DNA in a human body could fit inside one ice cube.

- Fastest-healing part of the human body: the tongue.

- Only joint in the human body that can rotate 360°? The shoulder.

- Right-handed people tend to scratch with their left hand, and vice versa.

- Every day about 10 billion tiny scales of skin rub off your body.

- Scabs are nature's Band-Aids. They start to form less than 10 seconds after you get cut, and they keep germs out while the cells underneath make new skin.

PIECES OF GALILEO

After he proved that the Earth was not the center of the galaxy, Galileo was condemned by the Catholic Church as a heretic. He died in 1642, but he could not be given a religious burial. So his bones were placed on a shelf in a church in Santa Croce, Italy. They sat on that shelf for a long time. In the 18th century, an admirer decided to hold onto a few of the great scientist's body parts—three fingers and a tooth. Then they placed his body in an elegant marble tomb. In 2010, Galileo's body parts went on display at the Florence, Italy, Museum of the History of Science. In 1992, the Catholic Church admitted that the judges who condemned Galileo had been wrong.

~~~→ FUN FACT ←~~~

A NEWBORN POOPS AND PEES OUT ITS OWN
BODY WEIGHT IN WASTE EVERY 60 HOURS.

Sometimes a celebrity's income doesn't depend on talent. It depends on body parts.

- **Ben Turpin.** He's believed to have been the first celebrity to insure a trademark feature. Turpin was a silent film star who had crossed eyes. If they had ever straightened, he would have received a $20,000 insurance payout.

- **Harvey Lowe.** In 1932, when he was 13 years old, Lowe won a national yo-yo contest. After the contest, he insured his hands for $150,000.

- **Jimmy Durante.** In the 1940s, he had his highly-recognizable nose insured for $50,000.

- **David Beckam.** The English soccer star has insured his legs for $70 million.

- **America Ferrera.** When the *Ugly Betty* star was hired to promote teeth-whitening products, her smile was insured for $10 million.

- **Mariah Carey.** Her five-octave singing range is worth insuring, but instead Carey insures her legs...for $1 billion!

~~~ FUN FACT ~~~

IF A COCKROACH TOUCHES A HUMAN, IT
RUNS TO SAFETY AND CLEANS ITSELF.

WHERE THE HEART IS: Think the heart is on the left side of the body? It's not. Crack open an anatomy book (or, if you're a doctor, crack open a human chest), and you'll see that the heart is more or less in the middle of the chest, between the lungs. So what makes people think the heart is on the left? The heart's left ventricle—a chamber that pumps blood—is larger than its right ventricle. This gives the heart its left-leaning shape. It also gives the sensation of the heartbeat coming from left of center. And why is the left ventricle larger? The right ventricle receives blood that's just come from the body and sends it off to the lungs to pick up fresh oxygen. The lungs are right next to the heart, so it's not a very long trip. But the left ventricle sends the oxygenated blood back to the rest of the body. Getting all that blood back to where it needs to go takes more muscle.

Zombie Boy

Think you're a strange and unusual person?
Read on to see how you measure up to this guy.

When Rick Murray was a kid growing up in Montreal, Canada, he I wanted to be...a Teenage Mutant Ninja Turtle. (We're not kidding.) He also wanted to live in the sewers like the fictional cartoon characters. That didn't happen, of course. What did? Murray fell in love with zombies and decided to become one.

To transform himself into a "zombie," Murray had his entire body covered with tattoos. Black ink surrounds his eyes. His "teeth" and "jawbone" can be seen beneath his cheeks. His "brain" appears from beneath his bald head. And his "guts," "skeleton," and several ghoulish designs are inked all over the rest of his body.

He's not done yet—Murray said he is also planning on removing one of his ear lobes to complete the look of the undead. (We hope *he's* kidding.)

TOP 7 ANIMAL BODY PARTS

Animals have some very useful body parts that people don't have. Which ones would you choose?

1. CLAWS: Humans got ripped off in the weapons department. Claws like a tiger? Built in can openers!

2. HORNS: With a pair of long, sweeping, super-pointy horns growing out of your head, you'd always have somewhere to hang your coat.

3. FLIPPERS: On top of making you a top-notch swimmer, flippers could turn you into a champion volleyball blocker. WHAM!

4. SPINNERETS: If you could produce webbing like spiders do, you could encase that annoying younger brother or sister in a soft, soundproof capsule that could then be stuck to the ceiling.

5. STINGER: The school bully just slammed you against your locker and demanded you hand over your lunch money...when ZAP! You shoot him with a paralyzing neurotoxin via your scorpion-like tail. Then you wrap him in spider silk and stick him to the ceiling beside your sibling.

6. ESCA: An esca is the thing that grows from the top of the head of an anglerfish. It acts as a lure to attract fish, which the anglerfish then eats in one terrifyingly fast and toothy gulp. If you had one of those...well, you could probably distract the lunch lady long enough to snatch an extra fish finger.

7. EXOSKELETON: Bones on the inside (an endoskeleton) help humans move around, but they don't offer a lot of protection. A hard shell on the outside—an exoskeleton—is like body armor, which would come in handy for playing football or hockey, or weathering a hailstorm. The downside? That outside armor does not expand as you grow. You'd have to shed it and wait around totally defenseless while your body makes a new one.

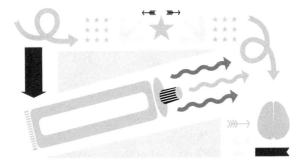

THAT'S THE MOST DISGUSTING...

- Earwax naturally forms little balls that drop out when you yawn, chew, or swallow.

- Hate to brush your teeth? Be glad you didn't live in Roman times. They used crushed mouse brains for toothpaste.

- When Eskimo babies have colds, their mothers suck the snot out of their noses.

- If your head is chopped off, your brain keeps working for about 15 seconds.

- It may not be ladylike, but the fact is, girls fart three times more often than boys.

- If stretched out, the longest tapeworm ever found in a human body would have been as tall as an 11-story building.

CHAPTER 20

LAST LAUGHS

~~~ FUN FACT ~~~

Q: WHAT'S THE FRENCH WORD FOR WALKIE-TALKIE?
A: TALKIE-WALKIE.

BIRD VIOLATES LANGUAGE LAWS

A customer at a Napierville, Quebec, pet shop threatened to report the shop to the Canadian government's French language monitoring office. Why? She was shown a parrot that spoke English.

A MOUSE JOKE: The Mouse family was making their way across the kitchen floor when the family cat rushed toward them. Daddy Mouse yelled, "BOW-WOW!" And the cat ran away. "That," said Daddy Mouse to his kids, "is why it's important to learn a second language."

THAT'S SO PUN-Y: A pun is a joke that plays on the multiple meanings of a word or the fact that there are words that sound alike but have different meanings. History hints that the lowly pun goes all the way back to ancient Egypt. Don't believe it? Surely you've heard of Cleopatra...the queen of denial. (Ouch.)

GRAVE HUMOR: Our crew of wandering BRI tombstone-ologists brought back these epitaphs and tombstone rhymes from the U.S. and Europe.

In Scotland:
Stranger, tread
This ground with
gravity:
Dentist Brown is
filling his last cavity.

In Michigan
Here lies
My horse Bill
If he hadn't died
He'd be living still

In England
Here I lie, and no
wonder I'm dead, for
the wheel of a wagon
went over my head.

In Mississippi
Once I Wasn't.
Then I Was.
Now I ain't Again.

In New York:
Harry Edsel Smith
Looked up the
elevator shaft
To see if the car was
on the way down.
It was.

In England:
Beneath this grassy
mound now rests
One Edgar Oscar Earl,
Who to another
hunter looked
Exactly like a squirrel.

- What do Eskimos use for toothpicks? Walrus whiskers.

- The praying mantis is the official state insect of Connecticut.

- What do people and lobsters have in common? Both like to eat lobster.

- The hairs on the butt of a cockroach are so sensitive that they can detect air currents made by the onrushing tongue of a toad.

- What do you call an ant that explodes when attacked? T-ant-T! (Okay. They're really called *Camponotus* ants, but that's not nearly as funny.)

- A pill bug can drink through its rear end.

> "Time's fun when you're having flies."
>
> —Kermit the Frog

COMIC STRIP WISDOM

Calvin: People think it must be fun to be a super genius, but they don't realize how hard it is to put up with all the idiots in the world.

Hobbes: Isn't your zipper supposed to be in the front of your pants?

SIGN LANGUAGE: Sometimes English translations on signs go really really wrong.

• **Sign in a Rome hotel room:** "Please dial 7 to retrieve your auto from the garbage."

• **Detour sign in Japan:** "Stop: Drive Sideways."

• **Sign in a Bucharest hotel lobby:** "The lift is being fixed for the next day. During that time we regret you will be unbearable."

• **Tokyo barbershop sign:** "All customers promptly executed."

Chindogu

Since the 1990s, writer Kenji Kawakami has been collecting odd inventions. He calls them chindogu, the Japanese word for "weird tool." These objects offer clever (and strange) solutions to everyday problems. But what makes chindogu really odd is that they are useless, impractical, or seriously embarrassing to use in public.

- **Portable crosswalk**
  Finding a safe place to cross the street can be a challenge. But now there's the Portable Crosswalk, a roll-up mat printed with white stripes. Simply choose a spot, unroll the fake crosswalk, and wait for the cars to stop so you can walk right through the traffic.

- **Hay Fever Hat**
  Got allergies? This headgear consists of a roll of toilet paper that sits on top of your head. It's held in place by a halo-shaped frame and a chinstrap. At the first sign of a sneeze, just reach up and pull off a few squares.

- **Wide-Awake Opener**

  No matter how boring school gets, this simple device will keep your eyes wide open. Attach the "gentle" alligator clips to your eyelids. Set the padded ring—attached to the clips with short tethers—on top of your head. The device will keep your eyes wide open.

- **Sweetheart's Training Arm**

  Basically, it's a fake arm and hand. It's made to dangle by your side as you walk down the street. Your boyfriend or girlfriend can hold hands with the fake hand until you stop being nervous and your palms stop sweating.

- **Automated Noodle Cooler**

  Stop burning your mouth on scalding noodles! This small battery-operated fan attaches to your fork, spoon, or chopsticks. It blows a cool breeze across the noodles as you bring them to your mouth. (Also works for soups and stews.)

- **Earring Safety Nets**

  These are little nets, similar to the kind you use to catch goldfish. They attach to the shoulders of your jacket or shirt and can catch falling earrings.

Britain may have more silly village names than any other place in the world. They include Fattahead, Giggleswick, Maggots End, Weeford, Butcombe, and Nether Wallop. When villages are subdivided, their names get even sillier, with results such as Great Snoring and Little Snoring. Finally, there's the English habit of naming the ends of villages "upper" and "lower." The upper end of one town is called Upperup. "If the hamlet grows anymore, we'll have to call one end of it Upper Upperup," joked a local historian.

Q: What animal didn't enter Noah's ark in pairs?
A: Worms. They came in apples.

FUNNIEST CROOK

"A Tampa, Florida, burglar who decided to rob a 24-hour convenience store didn't know the store was open 24 hours. He cut a hole in the roof, then fell through and landed on the coffee pot just as a police officer was buying some coffee."

—reported in *The Oregonian*

"Never stand between a dog and the hydrant."
—John Peers

"Never say 'Oops!' in the operating room."
—Dr. Leo Troy

"Never get into a battle of wits without any ammunition."
—Anonymous

"Never eat Chinese food in Oklahoma."
—Bryan Miller

"Never ask old people how they are if you have anything else to do that day."
—Joe Restivo

"Never try to tell all you know. It may take too short a time."
—Norman Ford

"Never try to use a cat's claw for a toothpick."
—Randy Glasbergen

"I'm not offended by all the dumb-blonde jokes because I know I'm not dumb...and I also know I'm not blonde."

—Dolly Parton

★ ★ ★ ★ ★ ★ ★ ★ ★ ★ ★ ★ ★ ★ ★ ★ ★ ★
★ ★ ★ ★ ★ ★ ★ ★ ★ ★ ★ ★ ★ ★ ★ ★ ★ ★
★ ★ ★ ★ ★ ★ ★ ★ ★ ★ ★ ★ ★ ★ ★ ★ ★ ★

LOL BUMPER STICKERS

Come to the dark side—We have cookies.

YOU CAN PICK YOUR NOSE AND PICK YOUR
FRIENDS, BUT YOU CANNOT WIPE YOUR
FRIENDS ON THE COUCH

**I used to have an open mind
but my brains kept falling out.**

My dog can lick anyone

TV IS GOODER THAN BOOKS

**Don't call me infantile,
you stinkybutt poophead.**

The Last Page

★

Fellow bathroom readers: Bathroom reading should never be taken loosely, so Sit Down and Be Counted! Join the Bathroom Readers' Institute. Just go to *www.bathroomreader.com* to sign up. It's free! Or send a self-addressed, stamped envelope and your e-mail address to: Bathroom Readers' Institute, P.O. Box 1117, Ashland, Oregon 97520. You'll receive a free membership card, our BRI newsletter (sent out via e-mail), discounts when ordering directly through the BRI, and a permanent spot on the BRI honor roll!

UNCLE JOHN'S NEXT
BATHROOM READER FOR KIDS ONLY
IS ALREADY IN THE WORKS!

Is there a subject you'd like to read about in our next Uncle John's Bathroom Reader for Kids Only? Go to CONTACT US at *www.bathroomreader.com* and let us know. We aim to please. Well, we're out of space, and when you've got to go, you've got to go. Hope to hear from you soon. Meanwhile, always remember to...

GO WITH THE FLOW!